Upper: Two interesting CDR vehicles photographed by John Langford at Strabane on Friday 14th August 1959. Trailer No 3, ex-Dublin & Blessington Steam Tramway Railcar, and Coach No 58, an ex-LMS Ballymena & Larne section luxury boat train coach. No 3 came to the CDR as a motorised vehicle, though spent its later years as a non-motorised trailer, as here. It survives in the museum at Cultra, while Coach 58's body, found in two sections in different parts of County Donegal, has been restored at the Donegal Railway Heritage Centre.
Lower: Railcar 18 also survived after assisting with the tracklifting at Donegal Town. Many years later, after doing tourist work at the Foyle Valley Railway in the 1990s, it was moved to Fintown Station, seen here in 2003, where for more than 10 years it has given visitors and enthusiasts a taste of a real ride on a CDR railcar for the 3 miles or so from Fintown towards Glenties. Photo by Neil Tee.

Top: Railcar No 16 at Stranorlar on 2nd April 1963, more than three years after closure of the line. In fact, as confirmed by the different layout of windows on the various passenger trailers, the power unit of 16 was here coupled to passenger trailer 15. Photo by Roger Joanes.

Middle: After serving as a holiday home for many years, Passenger Trailer 15 was rescued, though in rather poor condition, and resided in Edwin Kirk's yard at Drumstevlin, Donegal Town in 1995.

Bottom: After many years of efforts to find grant aid, Donegal Local Development Company provided funds to restore the body of Passenger Trailer 15. Here it is in use as a presentation room at Donegal Town shortly after work was completed in August 2013. Above two photos by Neil Tee.

Through the Hills of Donegal
An illustrated update on the history and current status of the County Donegal Railway
by Joe Carroll and Neil Tee
2nd Edition

CONTENTS

ISBN 978-1-874518-05-1

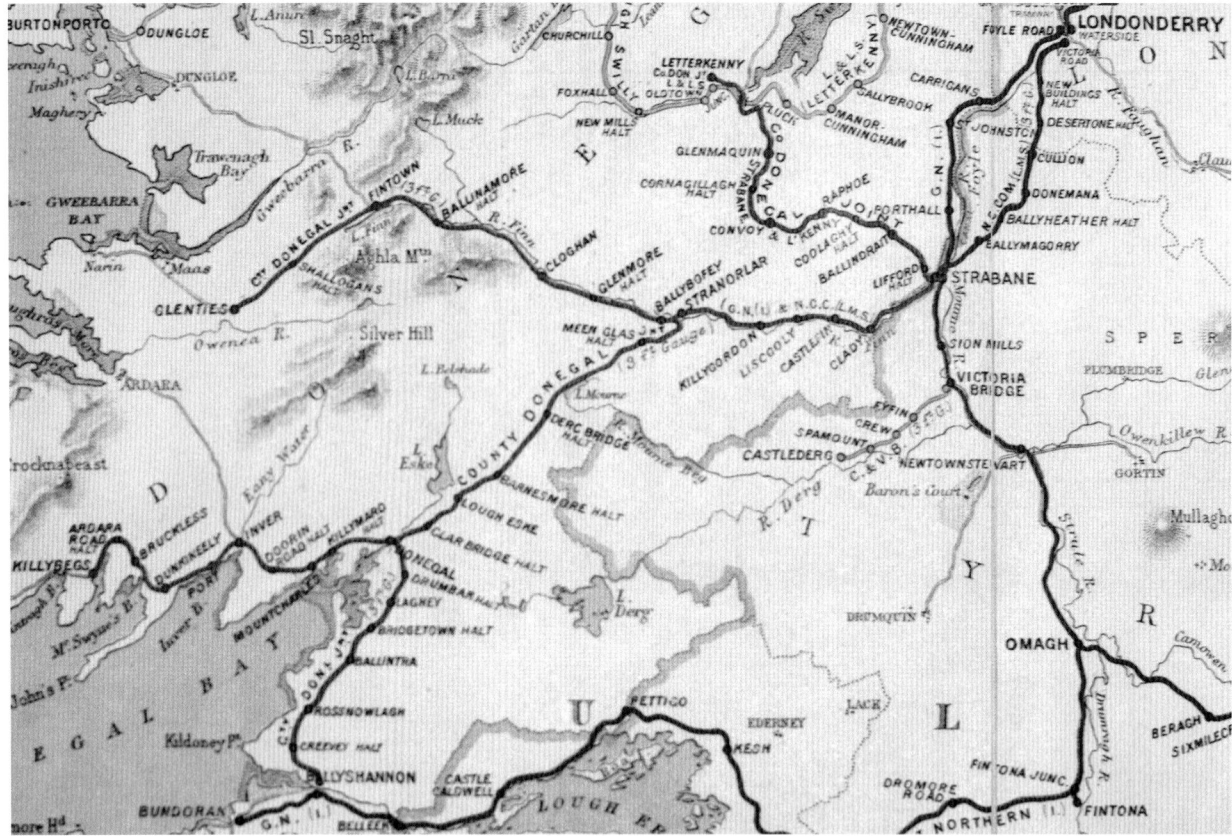

The extent of the County Donegal Railway in 1927 from a map of that time kindly lent by John Langford.

Introduction

This short review of the County Donegal Railways was first published in 1992. It was not intended to be a full history of the railway and the Joint Committee that ran it, but much more as a way of satisfying the curiosity of the many who see railway remains in County Donegal and wonder about the history, A definitive history entitled the County Donegal Railways was written by Dr E M Patterson and published by David & Charles, with editions from 1962, 1967 and 1982. After a period of being out of print and quite hard to obtain, a revised and extended edition was launched at Donegal Town in May 2014 under the auspices of Publishers Colourpoint. This work is essential for the serious CDR enthusiast. There are also a number of other publications, some having appeared since the first edition of our own work here, and a bibliography of these is provided on page 59.

We should like to like to extend our gratitude to all those who have in different ways assisted in the preparation of this book and its initial edition, in particular Steve Flanders for his design work, FAS who were associated with the resurrection of the old station in Donegal Town, the late Joe Curran – son of the railway's last general manager, Alan Corlett of the Isle of Man Railways, Mark Kennedy of the Ulster Folk & Transport Museum, the late Arthur Thompson from the North West of Ireland Railway Society, Hugh Dougherty and Dermot McCarthy. We would also like to thank all who provided photographs for this and other publications, past and forthcoming, by what is now County Donegal Railway Restoration Ltd, which grew out of the old South Donegal Railway Restoration Society. Many of the photographs were published for the first time in the 1992 edition. Photographs were provided by Hamish Stevenson, Hugh Dougherty, David Byrne, David Bell, David Carse, Seamus Clerkin, Geoff Oates, D M Lee, Jon Bailey, Hugh Davies, Roger Joanes, John Langford and the late Joe Curran.

Since the first edition of this work, County Donegal Railway Restoration Ltd has become established at the Donegal Railway Heritage Centre, with its museum and archive facility in the old station building in Donegal Town. As a result of the continuing work there more material has become available and the option to print some material in colour more feasible, and we trust that this new edition can provide the reader with more information and more impact than our first attempt over 20 years ago.

If you enjoy this book, and are interested in any other material about the County Donegal Railway or attempts to preserve sections of it, we do invite you to contact us at the old station in Donegal Town by post, phone, or email and through links on our web site, where you can find out more about the efforts to preserve artefacts and rolling stock from the railway and the drive to resurrect a working part of the railway which was such a key part of Donegal's rich transport heritage.

Joe Carroll   Neil Tee   May 2015

Top: Loco No 19 *Letterkenny* at Stranorlar, 27th September 1938, the only Class 5 loco to retain its original name and number after 1937, was scrapped in 1940. Dr Tucker - David Bayes collection. **Middle:** Donegal Town Station, Railcars Nos 18 & 12 prepare to leave. Note the three vans hauled by No 12 on the right. Adrian Vaughan Collection. **Bottom:** Back to Stranorlar in September 1938 again with no 11, *Phœnix*, on a freight train from Strabane, complete with 3rd-Brake-3rd coach. Late Canon Charles Bayes - David Bayes collection.

Top: On the closed Glenties branch, at the eastern end of Lough Finn at level crossing No 37, looking towards Fintown, before the track was removed in the mid 1950s. Photo by D M Lee. **Above:** Having been the first of the County Donegal Railway branches to close, part of the Glenties line was the first to be revived. Here, restored Railcar No 18 approaches Fintown alongside Lough Finn, about a mile west of the top picture's location, in 2005. Photo by Neil Tee.

I

The Rails of Donegal

When the Liverpool and Manchester Railway opened in 1830, it was thought to be a slightly eccentric novelty and damaging to the environment, but it was not long before railways began to spread throughout England linking cities and even villages together. Very soon any place not on the railway map was thought of as backward and was left behind the great rush towards the 'prosperity' of the Industrial Revolution

Ireland in the first half of the nineteenth century was becoming aware that its status in the British Empire was that of an under-developed rural economy and was determined not to be left out of the great railway race. Ireland's first railway, the Dublin and Kingstown (now Dun Laoghaire) Railway opened in

1834. By 1837, a section of track was laid between Derry and Strabane.

This was the first part of what was to become the Londonderry and Enniskillen line which was opened throughout in 1854. By 1861, Strabane and Derry were linked by rails to Belfast and Dundalk and, in Donegal, two Stranorlar-based landowners – the 4th Viscount Lifford of Meenglass Castle and Sir Samuel Hayes of Drumboe Castle - had seen the benefits of having a railway running to their part of the county and petitioned Parliament to be allowed to build one.

In May 1860 the Finn Valley Railway Act was passed and in the summer of the following year construction of a 5-foot 3-inch gauge line between Strabane and Stranorlar was begun. The fortunes and otherwise of the standard gauge Finn Valley Railway (FVR) are recounted eloquently by Dr E M Patterson in his book The County Donegal Railways and are outside the scope of this history.

By 1873 a shareholder of the FVR, a Mr Joseph Kerrigan, had begun calling for an extension of the line from Stranorlar to Donegal Town. Kerrigan's campaigning had aroused the enthusiasm of Lord Lifford and a separate company, the West Donegal Railway (WDR) was formed to build the Donegal link with Lord Lifford as chairman.

It was obvious from the ease with which government approval for the scheme was granted in 1874 that the building of railways in rural Ireland was set to reach epidemic proportions.

So that the new route should be completed at a reasonable cost a gauge of 3-feet was adopted. This gauge had been tried with success in Co. Antrim and was destined to become Ireland's other 'standard' gauge – over 550 miles of 3-foot gauge railway was eventually built.

The terrain through which the 18-mile line was to be built is mostly moorland and, to the east of the formidable Barnesmore Gap, was sparsely populated. In April 1880 the construction contract was awarded to Thomas Dixon at a price of £31,000 and by December of that year, 800 labourers were employed.

Severe weather that first winter brought work to a standstill for several months

Above: Lough Eske Station and Post Office, September 1952. Photo by D M Lee. **Below:** Railcar No 20 is turned at Killybegs on 27th September 1957. The base of the turntable was made from the frames of Class 5 loco No 19 Letterkenny. Photo by Hugh Davies, Photos From The Fifties.

and the problems of the WDR were compounded by the lack of enthusiasm of the Donegal townsfolk for the approaching railway. Funds ran low and it was decided to terminate the line at Druminnin Station, later known as Lough Eske, four miles from Donegal itself. Druminnin was opened in April 1882 and until the route was extended to Donegal seven years later passengers had to suffer the inconvenience of a 4-mile jaunt by horse car – hardly fitting for the discerning traveller of the 1880s!

The potato famine and the subsequent flood of emigration had left many areas in the west of Ireland with sparse populations. Strangely these areas became known as the 'congested districts' because the landholdings were too small and infertile to support the families living there. Several Acts of Parliament were implemented in the 1880s and

1890s to relieve the poverty and these 'congested districts' and some of these Acts involved building railways mainly to create jobs. The Light Railways Act of 1889 approved the extension of the WDR lines to the harbour town of Killybegs and to the small market town of Glenties.

Under this Act the proposed railways would be financed by the government but had to be operated by an existing railway company and the profits, if any could be generated, were to be divided equally between the two. With plans now in place for 43 more miles of narrow gauge railway, the standard gauge between Strabane and Stranorlar began to appear incongruous. The decision was taken to amalgamate the Finn Railway and the West Donegal to create the Donegal Railway Company and to convert the Finn Valley section to 3-foot gauge.

The GNR(I) made energetic attempts to halt this duplication of its route but the Derry extension of the Donegal Railway Company was approved in August 1896. The 14-mile track was built on the east bank of the River Foyle and, after several delays, was opened to traffic in 1900. By 1903 the Donegal was again approaching GNR(I) territory, at Ballyshannon this time where the GNR(I) had a station on its Bundoran branch.

Unlike Bundoran which was, and is, a popular seaside resort, Ballyshannon was a market town and in the early days of this century was a reasonably busy port. Shortly after the opening of the Ballyshannon branch the Donegal Railway Company was experiencing financial difficulties. The stage looked set for a takeover by the Midland Railway of Britain (later to become part of the London, Midland and Scottish Railway in 1923) which had already bought the Belfast and Northern Counties Railway and was anxious to expand its Irish operations. Naturally, the GNR(I) mounted frantic opposition to this proposed invasion of 'its' territory and the situation was finally resolved on May 1st 1906 when the Midland and the Great Northern became joint owners of the Donegal.

Above: Ballyshannon Station throat with railcar approaching, and trailer no 2 - ex Castlederg & Victoria Bridge Tramway - in yard. Base of water tower on right is still in place in 2015. Harold Eadie Collection. **Below::** Signal box, water tower and loco shed, Letterkenny, June 1950, now all disappeared. Photo by D M Lee.

The Killybegs extension was opened in 1893 and the following year the regauging of the Stranorlar-Strabane line was effected in just one weekend. The Glenties line finally opened in 1895 bringing the company's total mileage to 75½ miles of track.

The government grants had allowed the purchase of six new 4-6-0T locomotives (class 2), seventeen passenger coaches and some seventy-plus freight vehicles resulting in the Donegal Railway becoming a well-equipped and well run enterprise.

As most of the freight traffic for the system began or ended its journey at the port of Derry it was clear that the Donegal Railway would benefit by building its own terminus in that city and dispense with the tiresome transhipment of all freight (and passengers) to the 5-foot 3-inch gauge Great Northern Railway of Ireland [GNR(I)] at Strabane.

The new company was known as the County Donegal Railways Joint Committee (CDRJC) and three members from the boards of each owning company were appointed to the Committee. The Midland actually took control of the Strabane-Derry section but the rest of the system was operated by the Joint Committee.

Despite this unlikely partnership the CDRJC was very successful in running their railway and the company remained in existence until 1971.

On January 19th 1909 the final section of the Donegal railway network was opened giving a total route trackage of 124½ miles – the line from Strabane to Letterkenny providing the final 19 miles. Although owned by a separate company (the Strabane & Letterkenny Railway) investment was

Stranorlar, eleven years after closure, with the CDR headquarters building still in good condition. Unfortunately this building did not go on the record of protected structures, and was sadly demolished around 1980. Though perhaps arguable economically, this was an act of vandalism on railway heritage. Photo by Neil Tee.

made by both the GNR and the Midland and the line was operated by the Joint Committee at a cost of £3 10s 0d per mile per week.

At Letterkenny connection was made with the 99-mile Londonderry and Lough Swilly Railway by an exchange siding but the vast potential offered by joining the north-west of County Donegal with the main lines and therefore the rest of Ireland was never exploited.

The arrival of Mr Henry Forbes in 1910 to the posts of Secretary and Manager of what was now known as the County Donegal Railways Joint Committee (CDRJC or CDR for short) had a profound effect on the future of the company. Forbes was a railway man through and through and his almost fanatical dedication, courage and resourcefulness assured the survival of the CDR through many difficult years until his death in 1943. There are a wealth of stories and amusing anecdotes concerning Henry Forbes and interested readers are advised to consult the books and magazines listed in the bibliography at the end of this book.

In 1921 the 'Irish Free State' was formed and the CDR found that the new international border crossed their routes in several places. This 'international' status meant that, along with the Swilly and the Great Northern, the railway was not included in the 1925 amalgamation of the railways of the 'Free State'. It did however lead to many delays at customs points where the line crossed the border.

By the late 1920s the competition from private motor cars, buses and lorries was taking its toll on passenger and freight returns. Under Henry Forbes the CDR reacted by introducing railcars on passenger and light freight workings. These, among the first in the world, were initially petrol-powered. Later versions used diesel power and were the forerunners of the modern diesel-multiple units familiar on many railways.

After the death of Henry Forbes the management of the CDR was taken over by Mr B L Curran, a former accountant with the company. Despite Curran's very able efforts it was clear that much investment in the system was required to maintain a satisfactory service. By this time both the GNR(I) and LMS were nearing the end of their resources. Competition from the roads was also increasing in the immediate post World War Two years, and it was clear that some form of 'streamlining' was needed.

Predictably this took the form of closure of the uneconomic lines. The 24-mile route to Glenties was, unsurprisingly, the first to be affected with passenger services withdrawn in December 1947 and total closure following in early 1952. The Derry to Strabane line was next to fall in 1954, though the GNR(I)'s duplicate route on the western side of the River Foyle continued to link town and city for many years.

In 1955 the CDR applied to the Irish government for permission to close the Ballyshannon branch but was refused because of the parlous state of the Donegal to Ballyshannon road. However, in May 1959 permission was granted to close the entire CDR rail network and closure took effect on 31st December that year.

Some goods specials used the line until February 1960 and a driver, the late Joe Thompson, is reputed to have offered a 'ghost train' service between Donegal and Ballintra on the Ballyshannon branch until the management retook possession of his railcar.

So ended the proud history of a local railway company which served the scattered population of a rural community with dedication through many difficult years. The CDRJC continued in existence after railway closure, operating road, bus and freight services and was finally dissolved in July 1971 when all operations were handed over to CIE, the state-owned transport company.

Railcar No 10 at the sheds in Stranorlar in the 1950s. This was the "breaker of false teeth" referred to below. Its purchase was organised from the Clogher Valley Railway on the closure of that line in 1942 by the CDR General Manager of the time, Henry Forbes, who had been impressed by its articulated structure that set the trend for future CDR railcars. Railcar 10 also survived to the end of the CDR and can be found at the Ulster Folk & Transport Museum in Cultra. Photo by the late George Hanan.

Schooldays on the CDR

By Joey Cunningham

There are many memories of my years travelling daily to the Technical School in Donegal. One of them concerns a returning Yank. I will not use names as his relatives still live in Killybegs.

The day was fine and sunny, as are all days in our memories of youth, and the school pupils were travelling home on the afternoon service from Strabane to Killybegs which left Donegal about four. There was a large number of pupils getting on there, as youngsters from Killybegs and all stops up the line attended both the technical School and Clery's Secondary School in Donegal at that time.

That was in the late 'fifties and the rolling stock was being kept going as well as could be. Now I must explain for the benefit of those not into types of railcar that, when vehicles were out of service or there was a shortage for one reason or another, and there were no other options, a vehicle numbered 10 was taken out. Number 10 was very old and very short. In fact, it was so short that there were only doors at the front. Anyone who has seen pictures of Donegal railcars will recall that there were doors at the front and rear. Well no.10 was so short that it did not justify putting doors at the back and, as a result of the shortness, this railcar swayed and jolted much more than one of the longer ones.

The arriving yank had joined no.10 in Donegal, having come from Strabane in one of the bigger vehicles. Now in the back seat and talking loudly, as did Americans, this man commented on how jerky the ride had become on this part of the trip. We were now at Mountcharles and, as some of you may know, the speeds were not too fast on this stretch because of the gradients which were, generally, uphill.

After Mountcharles, the terrain became much more conducive to speed. Now, of course, speed is a relative thing considering that it took one hour to travel from Donegal to Killybegs. Then there would have been the condition of the track which, no doubt, was suffering from lack of maintenance and must have been deteriorating in those years. Anyway, our friend, as he had now become, was talking away to us, especially those from Killybegs, of which there were only a few. At some point on the line, I don't remember exactly where, no.10 took one or two violent lurches. Our visitor friend put his hand to his mouth and followed with a 'damn and blast' but in a much less distinct pronounciation than had been his usual delivery. You see, no.10 had broken the top plate of the man's dentures and, in those days, denture repairers or mechanics were as scarce as hen's teeth. So we can only imagine how the arriving Yank made his entry with such a faulty delivery – all thanks to no. 10. How could any form of transport today compare with that for adventure?

*From **The Phoenix**, magazine of the SDRRS, issue no.1, Summer 1991.*

Above: Railcar No 18 at Inver Station, 1957. This station is largely intact today after restoration by the Henderson family, although the wee signal box disappeared in the 1970s. The water tank is intact behind the road bridge.
Below: Railcar No 20 on a "Railway Enthusiasts Club" special charter stops for photographs in Barnesmore Gap, 1957. Above Photo by N C Simmons, below by Hugh Davies, both from Photos From The Fifties.

Top: One of the famous summer special excursions, 11 coaches long, is hauled back through the Barnesmore Gap from Rossnowlagh in July 1949. Photo from CDRRL archives. **Above:** Railcar No 14 at Strabane, September 1957, showing the bonnet sides raised for added cooling, a common expedient used by drivers. Photo by N C Simmons from Photos From The Fifties.

Top: Another steam-hauled excursion in the 1950s,in Barnesmore Gap this time double-headed - an amazing sight within the already dramatic nature of the scenery through which the line from Stranorlar to Donegal passed. Photo by the late Seamus Clerkin. **Above:** Inver Station from the platform, looking east towards Donegal town, showing the goods siding into which railcars reversed to allow trains in different directions to pass. Photo taken in September 1952 by D M Lee.

Above: Class 5A loco *Blanche* on the afternoon freight from Strabane to Lifford in September 1959. Note the good condition of the track at Strabane even though closure is a few months away. These freights on the Letterkenny line often has a good many wagons in the consist. Photo by Hamish Stevenson

II
Steam Locomotives

The first locomotive power units for the fledgling West Donegal Railway arrived from Sharp Stewart in 1881 and were to the 2-4-0T wheel arrangement.

Compared with later CDR designs these early Class 1 machines, as they were subsequently referred to, displayed a lack of power and their tractive effort of only 8,208 lbs limited them to trains of only about 110 tons over the Barnesmore Gap. It was with these engines that the Donegal began the practice of both naming and numbering its locomotives and the class 1 machines carried the names *Alice* (No1), *Blanche* (No 2) and *Lydia* (No 3) in honour of relatives of Lord Lifford, a major shareholder and proponent of the railway.

At the time of the introduction of the Class 1 locos the West Donegal Railway's territory only extended from Stranorlar to Druminin (later renamed Lough Eske) four miles east of Donegal Town and, as no telegraph was installed, in the early days the line was operated on the 'one engine in steam' principle.

The class 1 engines were adequate for their work but after approval was given for the Killybegs and Glenties extensions in 1890 it became evident that new, stronger engines with a better endurance were required.

By now the Finn Valley Railway and West Donegal Railway had amalgamated to form the Donegal Railway Company and it was in the name of that

company that an order was placed with Neilsen, Reid and Co. of Glasgow, for six 4-6-0T engines, though the cost was met from government funds as laid down in the 1889 Light Railways (Ireland) Act.

Six new locos

The class 2 locomotives (nos. 4 to 9) had a marked increase in power over their predecessors with 14 inch by 20 inch cylinders, a boiler pressure of 150 psi and a tractive effort of 11,900lbs but, because they could only carry one ton of coal, as the class 1 locos, and 650 gallons of water (500 gallons on the class 1 locos) their range was limited. Nonetheless, they were free-steaming engines and on average gave 37 years of service. The names of these class 2 locos were derived from a variety of sources: rivers, no.7 *Finn*, No 8 *Foyle*; houses of railway company directors, No 4 *Meenglas*, No 5 *Drumboe*; and villages in County Donegal, No 6 *Inver*, and No 9 *Columbkille*.

By 1927 four more classes of locomotives had been added to the fleet totalling 14 more engines and nos 5, 6 and 7 were withdrawn from service but, as they were cannibalised for spares to keep the remaining class 2 locos in traffic, they were not finally cut up until the mid-1930s.

A rare pair

The next additions to the Donegal Railway's loco stud were of the 4-4-4T type and the only examples of that wheel arrangement to work on narrow-gauge lines in the British Isles. The class 3 engines were the only Donegal locos to be fitted with a polished brass dome.

Named after two of the railway company's directors *Sir James* (Musgrave) and (Sir Samuel) *Hercules* (Hayes) nos 10 and 11 were delivered in 1902 by Neilsen Reid & Co., and had the lowest haulage capacity of any Donegal engine apart from the class 1s. Generally speaking nos 10 & 11 were not popular with the management and, when scrapped in 1935 and 1937, had by then lain idle for many years.

The Baltic tanks

The wheel arrangement of the next locomotives to join the Donegal Railway fleet, 4-6-4T (known as a 'Baltic' in Britain and 'Hudson' in the United States) was also unique on the Irish narrow-gauge lines.

They were delivered in 1904 by Nasmyth, Wilson & Co, of Manchester, who supplied all the later Donegal Railway engines. Designed with increased freight traffic in mind these forty-four-and-a-half ton machines did not, at first, live up to expectations and had a poor coal consumption.

During the period from 1912 to 1929 the Joint Committee's engineer Mr R Livesey carried out various modifications including the removal of a row of vertical boiler tubes and, later, fitting superheaters of his own design.

Above: Victoria Road Station, Derry. Class 5 Loco No 8 Foyle (formerly No 20 Raphoe) on the Strabane train in June 1953. Photograph by the late Canon Charles Bayes from the David Bayes collection.
Below: Class 2 Loco Meenglas. Photo by B H Jackson.

Both of these actions had a dramatic effect on the performance and economy of the Baltics and the class worked for many years. Originally numbered nos 12 to 15 the class was renumbered in 1937 as nos 9 to 12, though all retained their names recalling rivers in Co. Donegal: No 9 *Eske*, No 10 *Owenea*, No 14 *Erne* and No 15 *Mourne*.

In 1949 class 4 loco No 10 *Owenea* was involved in a fatal collision with Railcar No 17 at Donegal Town and was scrapped three years later: No 14 *Erne* was purchased for preservation in 1961, only to be cut up for scrap in 1967, allegedly in error, by the Hammond Lane Metal Co.

The Class 5 Locos

By the time the next class of loco arrived in Donegal the management of the system had been taken over by the County Donegal Railways Joint Committee.

Coming from Nasmyth, Wilson & Co, in 1907 and 1908 these 2-6-4T engines were initially non-superheated though their original satisfactory performance was enhanced in the 1920s when Livesey's patent superheaters were fitted. Weighing 43tons 10cwt these lively, free-steaming engines could haul a 130-ton load up a 1 in 40 gradient at 15mph and often coal consumption figures were as low as 29.5lb per mile. Their steam pressure, at 175 psi, was the highest of any Donegal loco type though their small water capacity of 1000 gallons did have the effect of limiting their useful range.

At first numbered 16 to 20, the machines in this class carried the names of Co. Donegal towns: No 16 *Donegal*, No 17 *Glenties*, No 18 *Killybegs*, No 19 *Letterkenny* and No 20 *Raphoe*. In the 1937 renumbering scheme the names and numbers of former class 2 locomotives were given to class 5.

Above: Class 5 loco No 6 *Columbkille* blows off steam at Strabane. Photo by N C Simmons from Photos From The Fifties. **Below:** One of the "Rare Pair" - Class 3 loco *Sir James* on turntable. CDRRL Archives.

Thus No 16 *Donegal* became No 4 *Meenglas*, No 17 became No 5 *Drumboe*, No 18 was named *Columbkille* (No 6), and No 20 changed to No 8 *Foyle*. Although No19 was to be known as No 7 *Finn*, the change was not carried out and it was as *Letterkenny* that this loco was scrapped in 1940. The class 5 engines were satisfactory machines and three of the class were bought by Dr Cox after the closure of the railway. Three locos, *Meenglas, Drumboe* and *Columbkille*, survive to this day.

The 'Big Engines'

While largely based on the design of the last 2-6-4T engines, the class 5A had many refinements and a larger water capacity than their predecessors.

The impressive specifications included 1500 gallon water tanks, Schmidt superheaters fitted with the new Livesey patent variable blast pipe, Boyer speed indicators, mileometer, pyrometer, smokebox ash

ejectors, Wakefield mechanical lubricators, and forced feed lubrication for axle boxes and bogie centres.

In an article in the Railway Magazine in 1912 the following comment was made of the Class 5A, 'with these engines an oil can is rather a luxury than a necessity. The cab is exceedingly roomy and all working handles (are) well arranged for convenience of working'.

The performance of this class matched the sophisticated design and in their prime, 5As could haul trains of 450 tons on level sections and 16-coach excursion trains through Barnesmore Gap (1 in 50) with ease. Primarily used on the heavy freight traffic on the Strabane – Letterkenny route, the 'big engines' remained in service almost until the end and No 2 *Blanche*, of the three still in service at closure, was bought by Belfast transport Museum.

These class 5A engines were originally named *Ballyshannon, Strabane* and *Stranorlar* and numbered 21, 2A and 3A though, in 1929 No 21 was renumbered No 1 and the other two had the suffix 'A' removed. At this time also, the names of the scrapped class 1 engines, *Alice, Blanche & Lydia*, were revived and applied to class 5A.

Visitors

The locos of the Irish narrow-gauge railways were often to be found on the tracks of other companies far removed from their original stomping ground.

Sometimes engines were temporarily leased or loaned though more usually moves were permanent. In this way the Cavan and Leitrim Railway's loco stud was boosted in later years from the Tralee and Dingle, and the Cork Blackrock and Passage railways.

As the CDR was not part of the 1925 nationalisation plan, and despite the exchange line with the Londonderry and Lough Swilly Railway at Letterkenny, most Donegal engines did not stray far.

Above: Bank Holiday excursion workings provided a rare chance for steam locos to perform passenger duties in the final years of the CDR. On August Bank Holiday Monday in 1959, Geoff Oates captured this view of Class 5A loco No 2 *Blanche* taking a breather at Ballyshannon. **Below Left:** Letterkenny Shed, 1957, Class 5 loco No 6 *Columbkille* gets steam up. Photo by N C Simmons - Photos From The Fifties. **Below Right:** Class 5A *Lydia*'s surviving nameplate at CDRRL's 2005 Festival. Photo by Neil Tee.

There were few visitors to the CDR system (though this was different in the case of the purchased railcars brought in from elsewhere) but there were also exceptions in the case of locomotives, both incoming and outgoing.

A Trip to Cork

In 1918, *Alice*, the last surviving class 1 2-4-0T engine was loaned to the Cork, Blackrock and Passage Railway, stopping for repairs in Inchicore works, Dublin, on the way. Her journey on a transporter wagon brought her through the territory of several 5 foot 3 inch gauge railways and, when in Cork, she proved useful and popular with the CB&P men. As *Alice* was 39 years old in 1920 and had cost £1195 when new it is surprising that the Joint Committee did not accept an offer of £400 made by the Cork company for the engine.

No.1 was returned to Donegal in 1921 and after damage suffered in Cork was repaired at a cost of almost £400. Five years of idleness at Stranorlar

followed and this, the last class 1 locomotive, was finally scrapped in 1926.

The only other CDR vehicle to make a long journey on 'foreign' railways was the ex-Derwent Valley Light Railway railcar no.2, which was driven over the entire L&LSR system by Ross Parks in 1927. This tour of inspection was in response to a request from the L&LSR that the CDRJC take over the running of their lines and create a narrow gauge system of 225 miles with centralised maintenance and management. The six members of the Joint Committee travelled the 99 miles of the Swilly company's track and were obviously unimpressed as it was decided that no further negotiations be carried out. Several years earlier, in 1922, Henry Hunt, manager of the L&LSR had tried to persuade Henry Forbes to allow one of the class 5A locos on to the Swilly's system as their management felt that they might purchase similar engines and were interested in an evaluation of the machines on their own territory.

Above: Class 4 locomotive No 10 *Owenea* shows the effect of the fatal collision near Hospital Halt outside Donegal Town with Railcar No 17 in August 1949. Note that the trailing bogie is "off the rails". No 10 was not repaired and was cut up in 1952. Photo by the late Seamus Clerkin. **Below:** A poor photograph but nevertheless showing Class 5 loco no 17 *Glenties* prior to her 1937 renaming as *Drumboe*, This loco has now been 60% restored by the RPSI under an Interreg IIIA grant obtained by CDRRL over the period 2006-8 and the RPSI has continued the restoration work. Photo from the late Conor Sinclair's Collection.

Forbes was loath to let his locomotives on to 'foreign' tracks and refused the request citing the 'Bogs of Drungloe' and the 'Irregulars of Burtonport '- the Irish Civil War was still in progress - as dangers to his engines. CDR goods and coaching stock did however find its way onto the Swilly from time to time and there were popular pilgrimage trains from Glenties and Killybegs to Doon Well near Kilmacrennan on the Burtonport Extension Railway. These were usually hauled from Letterkenny by L&LSR locomotives though the CDR did operate its own engines right through on several occasions between May 1931 and September 1939 according to the Late Willie MacGowan. Details of which

engines worked these specials have so far eluded us.

Contractors' locomotives

It was, naturally, during the construction of the various lines that were later to become known as the Donegal Railway that most of the few visiting engines appeared. These were the contractors' locomotives used for ballast trains and were probably fairly typical of their breed.

When McCrea and McFarland became the contractors on the Glenties extension in 1891 they brought with them Londonderry and Lough Swilly Railway loco no.1 named *J T Macky* after the Swilly

Class 5 loco No 5, *Drumboe*, at Strabane on 3rd September 1959, clearly showing the patching along the bottom of the side tank that was only repaired in 2006/7. Photo by Paul Booth.

chairman. This 0-6-2T was built in 1882 by Hawthorn, Black & Co., and was leased to the contractors who had previously used it for the construction of the Clogher Valley Railway in 1886. J T Macky remained on the Glenties line until its completion in 1895. The loco was scrapped in 1911.

Over on the Killybegs extension in 1891, contractor Thomas Dixon had bought a new engine from the Hunslett Co. This was named Bruckless when she was sold to British builders and was used on various contracts in England and Scotland.

Dixon also secured the contract to build the Ballyshannon extension in 1903 and this time used two locomotives on his construction trains. These were both 0-4-0 saddletanks from Hunslets. One was an old machine named *Isabella* and had an open cab, while the new model had been bought for the Ballyshannon job and was named *Coolmore*. *Isabella* and *Coolmore* were sold to Robert McAlpine & Co, when the Ballyshannnon line was opened to traffic and were to be used on the Strabane and Letterkenny scheme. McAlpines also purchased two new engines for this contract, both coming from Hudswell Clarke & Co. The first was an 0-6-0T named *Strabane* which came in 1907 and this was followed by an 0-4-0ST named *Donegal* in 1908. Photographs of the contractors' locomotives are very rare.

A giant at Stranorlar!

The most notable visitor to the CDR lines was one of the L&LSR's unique and impressive 4-8-4T engines. These powerful giants weighed fifty-eight and three-quarter tons in working order and had been delivered by Hudswell Clarke in 1912. In 1917, one of the pair of these engines (No 6) in this class, was towed to Stranorlar for boiler repairs in the CDRJC workshops at the request of the Irish Railway Executive Committee. No 6 was returned to Letterkenny under her own steam and continued to work on the Swilly until closure in 1953 when, after attempts to sell her as a running engine or museum exhibit failed, she was scrapped. The opportunity to save a marvellous narrow gauge work of art was missed.

In the very early years of the West Donegal Railway Lord Lifford, chairman of the company, was held in great respect and much admired for his dedication which had brought a railway to Donegal. Once on a fair day just as the last train of the evening was steaming slowly out of the station, slightly late, the guard, leaning out of his window, saw a man running across the rails. The guard heard the man shouting 'Lord Lifford is coming! Lord Lifford is coming!' The train was stopped and the class 1 engine backed her load smartly down the platform to await his lordship. The man who had shouted then walked up to a third class carriage, climbed in and, putting his head through the window, called out "Lord Lifford is aboard!"

Upper: The very first narrow gauge engine built for the Donegal Railway - Class 1 loco No 1 *Alice* - at Stranorlar in the early years of the 20th Century. This loco was at one stage loaned to the Cork, Blackrock and Passage Railway. **Middle:** Again in the early years if the 20th Century, the original Class 2 loco *Meenglas* at Stranorlar. The CDR worker near the smokebox is Sam Bingham, while the driver is thought to be Dan McCool. **Lower:** This is thought to be the original maker's photo of Class 5 loco No 18 *Donegal*, later renumbered as No 4 and renamed *Meenglas*. She is one of the three surviving members of this class in 2015, and currently stored outside the Foyle Valley Museum in Derry beside the Craigavon Bridge. All three photos from the late Willie McGowan Collection.

Upper: Class 1 loco no 2 *Blanche*. This maker's photo dates from 1881 and shows the 2-4-0T in lined works grey. Photo by B Jackson. **Lower:** In the 1950s the CDR was famous for its excursion trains. Here a double-headed excursion train in 1955 takes the Ballyshannon branch from Donegal Town headed by a Class 5A and assisted by a Class 5. A railcar and vans are visible near the water tower in the upper centre of picture. W McGowan Collection.

III

Coaching Stock

The first eleven three-foot gauge vehicles for the West Donegal Railway were purchased from the Railway Carriage and Wagon Company in 1882 and these proved adequate until extra traffic was generated by the 'government lines'- the extensions to Glenties and Killybegs - created the need for extra capacity. Consequently, in 1893, Oldbury of Birmingham supplied 17 extra vehicles, the cost of these being met from government funds.

The final route extensions to Derry (1900), Ballyshannon (1905) and Letterkenny (1909) brought 28 more new carriages into service and these proved to be the last new coaching stock purchased by the CDR. 13 of these vehicles actually belonged to the Strabane and Letterkenny Railway but in fact were used on all parts of the system. During the late '20s railcar operations began in earnest and scrappings and conversions to goods vans of the older coaching stock began at this time.

After World War Two the railcars carried virtually all passenger traffic apart from summer excursions and, because these put a strain on the now depleted coaching fleet, three second-hand vehicles were obtained from the Northern Counties Committee.

Six-wheel stock

All of the 1882 coaches were 31 feet long and ran on six wheels. No.1 of this batch was a First Class saloon carriage and in its later guise as the 'Directors' Saloon' became the only example of its class to escape conversion or scrapping and can now be seen in the Belfast Transport Museum. Nos. 2 to 8 all had five compartments and nos. 2 and 3 were tricomposites comprising third, second, first, first and second class compartments, respectively. Nos. 4 to 8 were all third class throughout, perhaps reflecting the expected traffic from the farming community. The last six-wheelers, nos. 9 to 11 were arranged as second, third, brake; and nos. 10 to 11 were eventually converted to goods vans in 1926 and 1927 becoming nos. 313 and 315.

Bogie coaches in 1893

These coaches were built by Oldbury for use on the extensions to Killybegs and Glenties and were perhaps the best of those bought for the Donegal railways. This class not only survived intact until closure but there are still existing examples: no.14 on the Foyle Valley Railway in Derry, and 3rd brake no. 28 which has been restored by County Donegal Railway Restoration Ltd (CDRRL) on display at Donegal Town.

Upper: Coach 13 at Ballyshannon on 21st August 1955. Photo by Michael Bunch. **Middle:** The same coach after the railway closed and it was in use as a holiday home in County Donegal. The three entrance doors on this side can still be seen. Photo from the Des McGlynn collection. **Lower:** One of the 1893 batch of coaches from Oldbury's was No 14, of the same design as No 12. No 14 was part of the Dr Cox purchase and happily can be seen today at the Foyle Valley Railway Centre, Derry. Photo by Hamish Stevenson.

Upper: Coach 28 at Strabane in the 1950s. After use as a holiday home following the railway's closure this was restored and is now on display in Donegal Town. Photo from CDRRL archives. **Middle:** Coach 30 at Strabane in the 1950s. This coach was fitted with roller bearings and regularly used as a railcar trailer, with the facility to connect to the railcar's electrics for lighting. Passengers liked the extra windows in the ends. Coach 30 survived closure and was rebuilt for display at the Foyle Valley Railway Centre in Derry. Photo from CDRRL archives. **Lower:** Coach 40, which had windows at one end, was one of those stored at Strabane in the 1960s ending up burned down to the frames by vandals. Photo by H Fayle from Harold Eadie Collection in CDRRL archives.

Upper: Coach 53 seen here at Strabane on in September 1959, was a sister to Coach 52. Photo from CDRRL Archives. **Lower:** Originally delivered as tricomposite coaches seating 48 passengers each, nos 55 and 56 were later converted to all 3rd-class and could then seat 60! No 55 was in Stranorlar in September 1952 when this photo was taken and was cut up at the end of that year. Photo by D M Lee. **Right:** Detail of Guard's ducket (lookout) on coach No 52, September 1952. Photo by D M Lee.

Coaches No 12 and Nos 14-17 each had five compartments comprising all three classes while No 13 uniquely had only three compartments; third, first, third. The central first class compartment was converted to a guard's section in 1953 and this coach lasted until the very end of the railway, finally being auctioned for use as a holiday home in 1961. Coaches nos 18-22 also had five compartments but featured only third class throughout.

The last of the 1893 Oldbury batch, nos 23 to 28, were all arranged as third-brake-third and had straight, matchboard sides. Guards' lookout duckets were fitted and 20 third class seats were provided, 10 per compartment. In 1901 Oldbury supplied six further vehicles, nos. 29 to 34. The first of these were two-compartment coaches with entrances through end verandahs which were panelled in by 1932. All these coaches were 36 feet long - the standard length of all later coaches.

A change of supplier

When fleet expansion was planned for 1905 nine coaches were purchased from Pickerings Ltd of Wishaw, Scotland. Two of these, nos. 39 and 40, were built with end verandahs, but as with nos. 29 and 30 these were later 'boxed in'. Four of the Pickering coaches had lavatories for the use of both first and third class passengers. As with most of the larger carriage orders, a number of third-brake-third vehicles were required and these were numbered 41 and 43.

Although the reason for the change of coaching stock supplier is unknown and although the Pickering coaches were good vehicles and lasted until the 1950s, there must be a logical reason as to why Oldbury was asked to supply the last thirteen new coaches bought by the Joint Committee in 1907. In fact, these vehicles were paid for by the

Strabane and Letterkenny Railway but, as they were operated and maintained by the CDRJC, some advice must have been given.

As usual the bulk of the order, nos. 44 to 51, was taken up by all third class compartment coaches and these seated 60 passengers. Nos. 52 to 54 provided the customary third-brake-third accomodation and had a guard's compartment that was 19 feet 2 inches long. The last two carriages in this batch, and indeed the last new coaches in the CDR fleet - nos. 55 and 56, could seat 48 passengers in six compartments.

Further notes on the coaching stock

At first no form of carriage heating was provided other than hot-water filled 'foot warmers'. By 1924, however, Henry Forbes, ever anxious for a bargain to improve his railway, obtained some second-hand steam heating equipment from the NCC Ballymena to Larne line and eventually most of the fleet was so fitted. Locos of classes 3, 4, 5 and 5a were altered to supply steam to the carriages.

Second class travel was abolished in 1924 and second class compartments were reclassified as third class. Three forms of carriage lighting were used by the CDRJC: Oil was in use until1912 when acetylene gas was introduced on all coaches,

One coach was fitted with electric light. This was no. 30 which had been converted to run on roller bearings for use as a railcar trailer in 1932. Power was supplied from the railcar batteries by jump leads. No steam locos were fitted with generators.

Several liveries were worn by the CDR coaches and the familiar red and cream colour scheme was introduced by Henry Forbes in 1937.

Top: Coach 56 escaped scrapping during the later years of the railway and was still in service when photographed here in Letterkenny in 1959 and was one of the coaches bought by Dr Cox in 1961. Photo by Hamish Stevenson. **Bottom:** Coach 58 was often used as a railcar trailer in the last years of the railway. Here it is parked ready for service on the old Glenties line bay at Stranorlar Station. Photo by Henry Emeleus.

Late arrivals

A shortage of passenger stock for use on the well-patronised summer excursions in the late 1940s led to the purchase of three second-hand bogie coaches from the NCC in 1951. Built for the narrow-gauge Larne to Ballymena boat trains in 1928, these coaches had standard LMS steel-clad sides fitted to narrow-gauge underframes and were originally provided with end corridor connections. On the boat trains they had been fitted with electric lighting and toilets, and were certainly the most luxurious coaches on the Irish narrow gauge.

At 50 feet in length nos. 57 and 59 (ex NCC nos. 352 and 351) were also six-and-half inches wider than existing CDR stock. The third coach, No 58, was only 41 feet long as, unlike the other two, it had been mounted on a shorter original 1879 chassis when reconstructed for the boat trains in the 1920s. All three coaches were treated to some modifications before entering traffic with the CDRJC. Running boards were removed, buffer and coupling heights were raised by ten-and-half inches, and the corridor connections were panelled in prior to acceptance trials on all sections of the line behind Railcar No.10.

The Miracle Coach

The NCC coaches lasted in traffic until the 1959 closure of the CDR. They were all auctioned off after closure. Because of transport difficulties - the same ones that had in fact prevented all the ex NCC modernised coaches from coming to the CDR in the 1950s, No 58 was cut into two before being towed to Dunfanaghy for use as two separate holiday homes. Over the years the two halves became further separated, going to different parts of the County. There is a happy ending here since one half was rescued by the Fintown Railway who initially used it as their ticket office at Fintown until its condition became too weather-beaten. In a praiseworthy display of co-operation they then donated it to CDRRL to await restoration - see top right.

The other half was discovered by CDRRL on the slopes of Muckish Mountain near Creeslough after a telephone call from a Scotsman in 2001 saying he had a 'railway wagon' in use as a holiday home and it was time expired. When the team went to see it, they recognised the signs of the original corridor connection - see middle right - and the length at just over 20 feet confirmed matters. Note how one of the original doors remained in use.

By the early 2000s both halves were in very poor condition bodily, and they were stored at CDRRL's headquarters at the Donegal Railway Heritage Centre. Shortly after its arrival, the Muckish half was inspected by the very railwayman who had raised the buffer beams, the late Cahill Hannigan of Stranorlar. It took another ten years to obtain a grant for restoration. After several unsuccessful appeals to the Heritage Council, Donegal Local Development Co agreed to sponsor the restoration of the remains of Coach 58.

This began with the re-welding together of the chassis parts, which remained in amazing condition for 133 years old. They were wire brushed, painted and no further work was needed other than welding back together the original 1961 cut, the work being shown arrowed in the photo above. A new body to match as closely as possible the coach's format in the 1950s was then constructed on the 1879 chassis and is in place acting as a major increase in display space for the Donegal Railway Heritage Centre, already being used for staging plays, for model railway shows and children's parties. The survival of this coach after being on different railways and then in two derelict halves is certainly something of a miracle.

IV

Freight Stock

As a country railway serving a scattered population, the 'Donegal" was quickly relied upon for the delivery of almost every commodity needed for daily rural life. There can be little doubt that the advent of rail transport in Co. Donegal contributed to a change in the fare available in the local shops as for the first time imported items such as sugar, tea, cloth (other than locally produced tweed, linen and wool) and, of course, Guiness could be transported inland from the ports of Derry, Killybegs, Donegal, Letterkenny and Ballyshannon both quickly and in quantity. The railways also meant that fishermen could get their catch to the markets in Belfast, Glasgow and Liverpool in good condition.

With the country's lack of mineral resources and the local availability of turf (peat) for domestic fuel the West Donegal Railway had little need for open wagons. So when the first order for freight vehicles was placed with Oldbury in 1881 the order consisting of just three open wagons, forty six-ton covered vans and two brake vans.

Further orders in 1893 and 1900 brought the freight fleet up to 239 vehicles by the time the County Donegal Railways Joint Committee was formed in 1906. Thirty-nine of these vehicles were open wagons belonging to the Strabane and Letterkenny Railway (a separate company whose traffic was operated by the CDRJC). Needless to say the S&LR wagons

were soon to be seen all over the CDR network. As built the first freight wagons had no vacuum brake and these were added during rebuilds.

Coach Conversions

The formation of the Irish Free State in 1923 saw the introduction of customs posts at Castlefin, Lifford and Strabane and the delays caused by customs clearance put a strain on the available wagon stock with as many as 20 wagons being held for examination on busy days.

CDR General Manager Henry Forbes, resourceful as ever, sought to overcome the shortage of freight vehicles by the simple expedient of converting life expired passenger coaches to covered goods vans. Both six-wheel and bogie stock was thus treated and as each vehicle had twice the capacity of an ordinary CDR van the situation was eased, temporarily at

Top: A selection of CDR vans at Letterkenny in the 1950s. Note the different heights and different styles with hinged doors and sliding doors. The rake includes a coach converted for freight use. **Above:** Built by Oldbury's in 1881 vans no 20 & 21 take a rest at Strabane in the Autumn of 1959, just months from closure. Note the differing roofs and the brake gear which was not fitted until the 1920s. Both photos by Hamish Stevenson.

least. Although the conversions were not as robust as purpose-built vans the policy was deemed successful and up to 1939 nineteen coaches were converted, some of them lasting in traffic until closure in 1959.

Tranship wagons

There were also twelve vehicles that had few equivalents elsewhere on the Irish narrow gauge system. These were the 'Tranship Wagons' (two covered and ten open) whose bodies could be transferred from their underframes onto other frames with 5'3" gauge running gear. Such 5'3" gauge vehicles were owned by the Great Northern Railway (Ireland) and transfer was effected at Strabane thereby allowing goods in CDR wagons to be moved to almost anywhere on the standard gauge system network.

The transfer system used rollers which were fitted to one end of the underframes only and the mixed gauge turntable at Strabane was used to prepare the wagons. At first loads of dressed stone from Mountcharles were the principal cargoes on these vehicles though even after the decline of this traffic the vehicles continued to be used and nos. 155 and 251 survived to the end.

Bogie stock

Apart from the converted coaches the CDR did not possess many bogie goods vehicles and in fact only purchased one of this type from new. This was no. 159 which came from Oldbury in 1900. All other bogie goods stock was bought secondhand from other three-foot gauge lines in the northwest. Bogie open goods stock came from the Castlederg and Victoria Bridge Railway in 1935 and the Clogher Valley Railway in 1941. A bogie low loader was obtained from the Northern Counties Committee in 1947. Costing £25 it was mainly used for oil storage.

Tank wagons

Nine tank wagons ran on the railway being also equipped with a buffer height part way between that of the CDR and that of the L&LSR, facilitating use on both. They were at least part-owned by the oil compnaies and not owned by the CDR until oil traffic ceased in 1954 when four were bought from Irish Shell and five from Esso.

Top: Van no 68 from the 1893 Oldbury batch seen in 1959. Note the recently replaced planks in the side panel and sliding door. The fine station lamp is, alas, no more. **Middle:** Stranorlar Station with its fine clock tower and adjacent church forms an excellent backdrop for bogie wagon no 334. This 15-ton wagon was bought from the closed Clogher Valley Railway in April 1942. **Bottom:** No 248 was delivered to the Strabane & Letterkenny Railway by Pickerings of Wishaw in 1907 and was classed as a combined goods, horse and cattle van. The ventilation flaps could be lowered to the open position when livestock was carried. All three photos by Hamish Stevenson.

Right: Loading mail into vans at Lifford. Prominent is van 332, converted in 1937 from 1893 Oldbury passenger van no 27 into a high capacity goods van. No 28 Oldbury coach however survives in its original form at the Donegal Railway Heritage Centre. **Lower Right:** Van No 1 - the first freight vehicle bought for the West Donegal Railway - was delivered in 1881 and was still in traffic four months before the system closed in December 1959. Both photos by Hamish Stevenson.

These had, in fact, been in traffic on both the CDR and the Londonderry and Lough Swilly Railway for a number of years under the original owners and were miniature versions of the tank wagons used on the British standard gauge lines. After purchase, the tanks were removed and the underframes converted to container flats or open wagons for their remaining CDR life.

The Red Wagons

A number of light wagons were acquired for use behind the railcars. The first of these came from the Castlederg & Victoria Bridge Tramway (C&VB). Later a batch of covered vans was obtained at the auctions following closure of the Clogher Valley Railway (CVR). Weighing just two tons the red wagons were introduced in an effort to get away from the practice of carrying passengers' luggage on the roofs of the railcars. A certain amount of disquiet was felt by Mr Arthur Hassard, the Irish railways inspector, over the use of these wagons and fiery correspondence flew between him and Henry Forbes for over two years. Eventually Forbes insistence on their safety and usefulness seems to have overcome the opposition and red wagons continued in use, in fact right up to closure of the system.

Restorations

Grants from both the Heritage Council and Interreg were used to obtain, stabilise and then restore a number of remains of rolling stock items. Pictured at right is the restored Oldbury sliding door van 84 which had been discovered in Killybegs and moved to the Foyle Valley Railway. During storage there it was burnt out by vandals but then restored by CDRRL under an Interreg Grant. It is pictured at Donegal Town needing only new wheel bearings to return to traffic. Also pictured is the restored body of Red Van 12, right, found in a garden in Castlefinn, and also restored by CDRRL under an Interreg Grant, using parts from Red Van No 10 found in a field near Strabane. Both Grey Van 84 and Red Van 12 are on display currently at the Donegal Railway Heritage Centre.

V

The Rise of the Railcars

While the motor lorry and road bus had proved their value during World War One and quickly became common sights on the roads of Britain, it wasn't until the late 1920s that the Irish rural railways began to feel any threat from that quarter.

In the north-west of the country the three railway companies first saw danger from the road buses, which were far more flexible in operation than steam-hauled trains. The Great Northern Railway of Ireland and the Londonderry and Lough Swilly Railway sought to counter the threat to their passenger figures by entering the field of road bus operations and, where possible, by buying out their competitors. Both concerns were very successful in their ventures and the GNR(I) continued bus services until it was finally absorbed by CIE in 1958. The Lough Swilly Company continued to operate a number of bus routes until April 2014. The CDR also experimented with road bus operations from 1930 to 1933 but the main thrust of their counter-offensive in the fight to win passengers was rail based.

The Railmotors

Whereas steam trains could haul heavy loads at relatively high speeds between stations a convenient distance apart, road buses could stop anywhere to set down or pick up even one passenger without undue cost. To the Joint Committee it was obvious that a rail vehicle with the versatility of a bus was needed and furthermore, they knew just the type of vehicle required.

Back in 1907 an open 'Inspection Car' had been purchased from Allday and Onions of Birmingham which, by 1926, had been fitted with a Ford 22hp petrol engine and a closed body with seating for six. Pressed into service on the mail run from Stranorlar to Glenties during the coal strike of 1926, the "Railmotor" soon proved its usefulness and paved the way for future railcar operations on the CDR.

In 1949 the Railmotor, numbered '1' in 1927, was again re-engined and lasted in service until closure in 1959. Initally preserved by the old Belfast Transport Museum, No.1 can now be seen in the Ulster Folk & Transport Museum in Cultra along with a significant amount of other Donegal machinery.

Further Developments

Emboldened by the successes of the 'Railmotor', Henry Forbes began the hunt for larger petrol railcars and set his sights on a pair of Ford-engined units which were being offered for sale by the Derwent Valley Light Railway in Britain. The manager of the Kent and East Sussex Railway, the redoubtable Colonel Stevens – as renowned as Forbes in his resourcefulness and dedication to his railways – also bid for the cars and Forbes was forced to offer £480, almost £100 more than he had hoped to pay, to secure the vehicles.

After further problems with the Free State customs, it was decided that the railcars should be classed as road buses and that duty of £166.8s.7d was payable – this was later returned to the Committee after some correspondence from Forbes. The railcars were altered at the Dundalk works of the GNR(I) by narrowing their gauge and lowering the bodies to suit the Donegal lines.

By the end of October 1926 both railcars, now numbered 2 and 3, had entered service and were covering about 2400 miles each per month on the Glenties

Top: Railcar No 1 with Trailer 5 at Stranorlar. Photo from the Harold Eadie Collection. **Bottom:** Railcar No 2, ex-Derwent Valley Light Railway, at Stranorlar in July 1931. This vehicle was in CDR service between 1926 and 1934. No 2 and her sister No 3 were described by a certain senior Dundalk engineer as "clocking" (ie broody) hens. No 2 certainly looks like she is ready to sit down onto a nest of eggs! This photo of No 2 at Donegal Town from the Sam Carse collection - courtesy David Carse.

branch (No 2) and the Finn Valley and Letterkenny sections (No 3). The DVLR railcars did have their share of teething troubles but gave good service until they were withdrawn in 1934.

In 1928, however, Railcar No 4 was built for the CDR at the GNR(I)'s Dundalk works. This vehicle was based on a 30cwt Ford lorry chassis and had a body built by O'Doherty coachbuilders of Strabane. No 4 was fitted with seating for 21 passengers and originally had two entrance doors at the front, though the offside door was later moved to the rear thus reducing the seating by one place. Initially, the Ford chassis suffered a number of broken axles but once stronger materials were used things settled down and No 4 remained in service for 19 years.

No 5 in the railcar series was a trailer (see pages 36 & 61). Like No 4, Railcar No 6 also came from the Dundalk GNR(I) works with O"Doherty bodywork in 1930, but was quite heavy for its time at five-and-a-half tons and ran on six wheels. A second-hand Reo 32hp petrol engine provided the power and no.6, "a most comfortable vehicle to ride in", gave excellent service until 1945 when the engine was removed and the car rebuilt as a trailer. In this form no.6 was used until as late as 1958.

The Coming of Diesels

In 1930 the decision was taken to power the new railcars, Nos 7 & 8, with Gardner 6L2 diesel engines. This was the first time diesel railcars were used for passenger services on a regular basis in the British Isles. In Germany, however, advances were being made with diesel traction. So much so that, in 1932, a 93mph service was set up between Berlin and Hamburg. Using two-car units this service was known as Der Fliegender Hamburger (The Flying Hamburger) and operated successfully until the outbreak of World War Two.

Top: During its 19 years of revenue earning service No 4 had its entrances altered and a rear door was fitted to the off side. It is seen here in company with No 14. Both photos from Sam Carse collection - courtesy David Carse. **Middle:** Diesel Railcar No 7 and driver at Donegal Town in 1939. The ugly look of this first diesel railcar in the British Isles was because the diesel engine was too wide to allow the front axle to go under the bonnet, and it had to be placed on a pony truck ahead of it. This historic vehicle was scrapped in 1949. At a show held in Donegal Town station in August 2014, CDRRL staff were delighted to meet 92-year-old Driver McAuley who had driven its twin Railcar No 8 and most of the later railcars in his long career with the CDRJC. Photo from CDRRL archives. **Bottom:** Railcar no 12 at Killybegs showing the fine overall roof and the oil depot beyond. Photo by John Langford.

The Donegal railcars were tested to a maximum speed of 43mph and on a run between Ballyshannon and Stranorlar gave a consumption of 25mpg. Drive from the forward-mounted engine was taken through a Thornycroft gearbox to the two rear axles, which were linked by a drive chain, and the front axle was supported on a pony truck which protruded in front of the radiator. Nos. 7 & 8 spent most of their 18-year lives on the Ballyshannon branch and their success led to the use of diesel engines in all future railcar designs. Unfortunately, despite their significance in the development of diesel railcars neither was preserved.

Indeed the next two railcars in rhe numbered series were converted CDR road buses with petrol engines, No 9 and the first No 10. For the second No 10 and No 11 on fashion reverted to diesel, see pages 40 & 41.

The Articulated Railcars

We will now look at another innovative vehicle which also influenced the design of all subsequent CDR railcars. This was Railcar No 12 and was built for the CDR by Walker Bros. of Wigan and the GNR(I). No.12 differed from previous cars in that she was based on an articulated system first used on the Clogher Valley railway in 1932. Henry Forbes was a member of the Committee of Management set up to run the CVR and was impressed with their first railcar.

On the CDR vehicle the Gardner 6L2, 74hp engine and the driving cab were housed on a 'power bogie' while the coach body was trailed behind on an unpowered bogie and could seat 41 passengers. No.12 cost £2,281 in 1934 and, as she covered almost one million miles in CDR service, may be seen as the best vehicle ever owned by the Joint Committee. Now over 80 years old, No.12 still survives stored in working order at the Foyle Valley Railway Centre in Derry.

Top: Railcar No 4, seen here at Stranorlar, was the first new railcar on the CDR and arrived in 1928. **Middle:** Railcar No 14, noted for its curved upper window frames, at Donegal Station, June 19th 1957. Photo by Geoff Oates - Tony Ward collection. **Bottom:** Railcar Trailer 13 photographed at Stranorlar on 27th September 1938. This small trailer was converted from a Ford-engined railcar originally owned by the Dublin & Blessington Steam Tramway and purchased by the CDR in 1934. It was scrapped in 1944. Photo by the late Canon Charles Bayes from the David Bayes Collection.

Top: Drewry Petrol Railcar No 3 (ex Dublin and Blessington Steam Tramway) at Strabane in 1935 when it still had its own motive power. It took over the number of the previous No 3 (the "clocking hen") in 1934 and was subsequently rebuilt as a trailer in 1944, following which it survived to the end of the railway in 1959 and now resides in the Ulster Folk and Transport Museum in Cultra, Belfast. Photo from the John Langford collection.

Middle: Built by O'Doherty, coachbuilders of Strabane, and the GNR(I) works at Dundalk in 1930, Railcar no 6 was the last of the CDR's petrol-engined railcars. It is seen here at the attractive Glenties Station on 15th July 1931. The building happily survives. Photo from the Sam Carse Collection, courtesy David Carse.

Bottom: CDR Railcar No 15, first of the full-cab models, on Killybegs turntable in September 1959. The turntable has gone now, but is commemorated in the Turntable Bar of the Tara Hotel whose rear entrance is beside the turntable site. No 15's articulated passenger unit survived many years of storage in the open, and can now be seen restored, albeit without wheels, at the Donegal Railway Heritage Centre, see page 4. Photo by Mike Schumann.

Railcars Nos 14 and 15 arrived in 1934 and 1935 respectively. They were broadly similar to No 12, though No 15 had a more modern full-width cab, and, like No 12, both carried 41 passengers. During their lives they worked all over the system and travelled over 850,000 miles each. Surviving to the end they were auctioned in 1961.

Slightly heavier than their predecessors, Railcars Nos 16, 17 & 18 were powered by a Gardener 6LW, 102hp engine. As before, the combination of Walker power bogie and GNR(I) body was utilised with great success and Nos 16 and 18 survived until closure. Railcar No 17 was destroyed in a collision with locomotive no 13 Owenea outside Donegal station in August 1949, in which three people lost their lives. Nos 16 and 18 were purchased by Dr Cox in 1961 and, though No 16's tractor unit was was cut up for scrap after lying at Stranorlar for over a decade after closure, No 18 was spared and is now owned by the North West of Ireland Railway Society and running on the Fintown Railway.

Railcars – the final development

The last railcars built for the CDR were delivered in 1950 (No 19) and 1951 (No 20). Built to an advanced design with the cab fully enclosing the engine they looked distinctly more modern than even Nos 16 to 18. Four similar railcars were built for the West Clare Railway. The 102hp Gardner engine was again used and the Dundalk body featured windows in anti-shock panels and an 'Airvac' ventilating system. As the CDR rail services were withdrawn when these cars were less than ten years old they were quickly bought intact by the Isle of Man Railway Co. in 1961. They were initially used on the line from Douglas to Peel before that closed. Subsequently a major restoration project was started but the work has been suspended due to limited funds. However when viewed in 2003, the quality of the work done so far seemed excellent.

Trailers

As the early railcars were withdrawn from traffic some were rebuilt as trailers and often remained in service for many more years in this form.

Other vehicles were built or bought as railcar trailers and, being lightweight, gave a useful increase in carrying capacity to the first railcars. Henry Forbes was writing to G T Glover, Engineer of the GNR(I), as early as 1926 advocating the use of 30-seat trailers with railmotor no 1, but it was not until June 1929 that Trailer No 5 arrived.

A body by O'Doherty's of Strabane was built on a chassis from Knutsford Motors Ltd, and this could carry between 29 and 31 passengers - reports vary. Weighing only three-and-a-quarter tons No 5 cost £318 and saw service until the end of the railway when it was sold for use as a ticket office or changing room at Donegal football ground. By June 1965 it was in use as a caravan at Rossnowlagh, a set of road wheels having been fitted.

In 1934 another trailer was added to the fleet. This was originally a railcar on the 5'3" Irish standard gauge Dublin and Blessington Steam Tramway and was powered by a 22hp Ford petrol engine. Numbered into the railcar series as No 13 she was regauged at Stranorlar when the engine was removed and she was then used as a trailer until 1944. As mentioned earlier, Railcar No 6 also had its petrol engine removed, in 1945, when converted to a trailer.

There were three other vehicles in the railcar fleet but, as they all started life on other railways, these will be considered in the chapter on imported stock.

Conservation & Preservation

A remarkable amount of the Donegal railcar material has survived. We have seen that No 1 is in the museum at Cultra, where it accompanies No 10. No 12 is at the Foyle Valley Museum in Derry, and No 18 is in working order at the Fintown Railway. Nos 19 & 20 remain semi-restored and out of use at Douglas on the Isle of Man.

Railcar Trailer 5 was secured for restoration in the Summer of 1994. It was discovered by local photographer the late Conor Sinclair at Doochary, near Fintown, Co. Donegal. Following its time with Donegal Football Club it was originally believed that Trailer 5 had been scrapped in the mid seventies but it had actually been towed to Doochary for use as a holiday home. Incredibly it surrvived and in 2006-7 received a full body restoration at the Railway Preservation Society of Ireland premises in Whitehead, Antrim. This included new roof timbers and felting to make it watertight. The doors have been remade using the original patterns. The restoration effort was financed with the help of an Interreg IIIA European cross-border grant. Trailer 5 is now in use at the Donegal Railway Heritage Centre as an exhibition and meeting room.

The maintenance staff at Stranorlar were known to swap around the passenger trailer of the railcars to minimise inconvenience when maintenance was needed. What was thought to be Railcar 16 spotted at Stranorlar on the abandoned trackbed as late as 1971 was in fact the power unit of 16 fitted to No 15 trailer as confirmed by the different type of top-light windows fitted to No 15. Some years later Railcar Trailer 15 was found in use as a holiday home. It spent 15 years in store in Donegal Town before a Heritage Grant allowed a base to be constructed for it to stand on at the Donegal Railway Heritage Centre. A Donegal Local Development Company (DLDC) grant then provided the funds to restore the body. New uprights and roof supports were made by the Railway Preservation Society of Ireland, then local Donegal joiners and metal workers, ably assisted by Donegal Railway Heritage Centre staff, completed the rebuilding so that the vehicle could function as a presentation room. Restoration of the passenger trailer of No 15 wascompleted in 2013 at the Donegal Railway Heritage Centre and it is in use as a presentation and function room there.

Top: The interior of Railcar no 12, looking towards the rear end. The seats are actually somehwat narrower than in a standard service bus. Photo by the late Conor Sinclair. **Bottom:** Railcar No 12 at Stranorlar in 1958. Railcar No 12 survived closure and is now at the Foyle Valley Railway Centre in Derry. In the late 1990s Railcar 12 was in running order and used to take tourists along the 3 miles of 3-foot gauge line leading south from the Centre along the old GNR(I) trackbed towards Strabane. Sadly this practice has now ceased. Photo by the late Seamus Clerkin.

Top: Railcar No 14 and loco No 6 Columbkille at Letterkenny in 1957. **Middle:** Railcar No 15 shunts vans outside Ballyshannon good shed in 1957. Both above photos by N C Simmons from Photos From The Fifties. **Bottom:** Railcar 16, a full-cab version, trailer (consisting of a passenger coach) plus van (attached at Raphoe) forming the 8.45 am Letterkenny to Strabane service awaits the customs check at Lifford Station, 17th September 1957. Photo by John Langford.

Left: Railcar No 20 complete with two vans delivers the mail under the overall roof of Killybegs Station during the 1950s. Photo by N C Simmons

Middle: Railcars 19 & 20 at Donegal Town, 1957. This photo shows the various differences in window detail and livery between these two cars. Photo by Hugh Davies

Bottom: Although not a railcar, Phœnix was numbered 11 in the railcar series. This photo showing the "ugly" end while Phœnix shunts vans to a railcar at Strabane. Photo by N C Simmons. All above photos from High Davies' Photos From The Fifties collection.

VI

Imported Rolling Stock

With Henry Forbes at the helm, the CDRJC continued to survive, if not exactly prosper, through World War One, a coal strike, the Depression and the rail strike of 1933. The joint owners of the Donegal Railway, the Great Northern Railway (Ireland) and the Northern Counties Commission of the London, Midland and Scottish Railway of Britain, were not always able to provide funds for the renewal of equipment and the Stranorlar depot fitters became skilled at 'make do and mend'.

Forbes had a nose for a bargain and followed any lead that could help him improve the lot of 'his' railway. It had long been common practice that a railway would buy and make good use of equipment that was of no further use to another. As reported earlier, railcars nos. 2 and 3 were obtained in this way from the Derwent Valley Light Railway, but when these cars were withdrawn two other vehicles took the numbers of the SVLR railcars.

The Second No 2

Not far to the east of Stranorlar, just inside Co.Tyrone, the town of Castlederg was served by a seven-and-a-quarter mile long three foot gauge tramway which connected with the Derry-Enniskillen section of the GNR(I) at Victoria Bridge.

Although it relied mainly on steam traction, the Castlederg and Victoria Bridge Tramway had built a railcar in 1925 to an in-house design. Powered by a 20hp Fordson TVO paraffin engine, the little vehicle

served for only three years and was in a poor state when viewed by Henry Forbes in 1932. After the usual correspondence and bargaining a price of £25 was agreed and the derelict railcar was taken to Stranorlar where a 22hp Reo engine was installed.

As railcar no.2 it entered traffic in 1934 and appears to have given a reasonable service until 1941. In 1944 the engine was removed and a new body fitted and, as trailer no.2, the vehicle survived until the end of rail services. As the auction it was sold for use as a private children's library at Mountcharles. In 1991 all that remained on site were a pair of folding doors.

The Drewry Railcar, No 3

When trailer no.13 had been obtained in 1934 from the Hammond Lane metal Co – Ireland's largest scrap metal dealer – another vehicle was also purchased, again from the stock of the then defunct Dublin and Blessington Steam Tramway (D&BST). This was a 35hp Drewry petrol-engined eight-wheeled railcar. Delivered in 1934 and regauged by placing the wheels inside the journals, rather than outside as on the five-foot three-inch gauge D&BST, this was the only railcar on the CDR that could be driven from either end and it is perhaps surprising that some of the later purpose-built vehicles did not have this feature.

With a seating capacity of 40, no.3 (the Drewry inherited this number from the withdrawn DVLR vehicle, see page 32, and, in fact, coincidentally had the same number on the Blessington System) was a most useful addition to the fleet and after the removal of the engine in 1943 was rebuilt as a trailer, eventually becoming part of the Belfast Transport Museum collection in 1960. No.3 is currently on display at the Foyle Valley Railway Centre in Derry.

A Pioneer Joins The Fleet

As mentioned in a previous chapter, railcar no.12 and all subsequent railcars were direct descendents of an articulated vehicle that had been observed on the Clogher Valley railway in 1932. When the CVR finally surrendered to the competition from the roads in 1942 – tramways were often more vulnerable than true railways – it was not surprising that the pioneer articulated railcar was bought by the CDR, becoming No 10 in its own fleet.

The power bogie was similar to that of no. 12 fitted with a Gardner 6L2 diesel, though the body could only seat 28 passengers. Owing to its shorter wheelbase this car was said to be less comfortable than its larger sisters. Nevertheless it continued in use until closure and was then bought by the Belfast Transport Museum

Trailer No 2 which was once a Fordson-engined railcar on the Castlederg and Victoria Bridge Tramway. After service with a new engine on the CDR, it lasted as a trailer until closure. Here it is at Ballyshannon on 16th August 1959. Photo by John Langford.

Phœnix, the CDR's unique diesel shunter, which was converted from an Atkinson-Walker steam tractor in 1932. It is seen here moving a short freight train at Strabane on September 12th, 1959. *Phœnix* survives to this day and may be seen at the Ulster Folk and Transport Museum at Cultra. Photo by Hamish Stevenson.

which has now been replaced by the Ulster Folk and Transport museum at Cultra where Railcar 10 is now on view.

The Phoenix Rises

During the first 150 years of Irish railway history a number of weird and wonderful machines took to the rails on all gauges (or even no gauge at all in the case of the Listowel and Ballybunion Monorail) and, sadly, most have now disappeared.

The double-ended steam locos of the Dublin and Blessington Steam Railway matched by their double-decked coaches, the Drumm battery railcars, O V Bulleid's giant and unsuccessful turf-burning steam loco for CIE, and Guinness's one-foot ten-inch gauge little steam locomotives that could be hoisted up to become a standard gauge shunting loco, had few equals in Europe. Strange conversions were also tried out such as the GNR(I) railbuses which were a standard road bus fitted with steel railway wheels and having pneumatic tyres. The CDR, that expert in improvisation, had one vehicle that sits comfortably in these ranks and which must also be regarded as a successful conversion. That unique vehicle is *Phœnix*. Is, rather than was, because *Phœnix* has survived into preservation.

In 1929 the Clogher Valley Railway acquired an Atkinson Walker class A3 steam tractor. With an impressive specification the vertical-boilered machine was expected to prove very useful but, alas, after only nine months in service it was deemed a total failure. Failure also affected the Atkinson Walker company which soon after went into receivership thus ending the CVR's chances of refund.

Being a member of the Committee of Management of the CVR, the Donegal's Henry Forbes was familiar with the steam tractor and hoped to buy it for his railway. After consultation with Mr Glover, the engineer of the GNR(I), it was decided that a diesel engine could be fitted to the machine and a purchase price of £105 was negotiated.

The steam tractor was taken to Dundalk and steam machinery was removed and a Gardner 6L2 engine was installed. The original side tanks were retained to hold the fuel and cooling water and the exhaust was taken to a silencer on the roof.

In December, the vehicle was delivered to Stranorlar to begin acceptance trials. Because the 'steam' tractor had undergone a transformation and been granted a new lease of life. Forbes had it named *Phœnix* and it was numbered no.11 in the railcar series.

Phoenix was slow and noisy and its haulage capacity on 'inter-town' trains was limited but, nevertheless, it was deemed a success and performed its usual task of shunting wagons for customs examination of Strabane, Lifford and Castlefin with ease.

On the closure of the railway *Phœnix* was used to lift the rails on the Strabane and Letterkenny section before purchase by the Belfast Transport Museum and can now be seen at the Ulster Folk and Transport Museum in Cultra, just east of Belfast.

Incidentally, it is understood that the boiler removed from Phœnix in 1932 was sold to a local laundry – for £100! Henry Forbes certainly knew how to strike a bargain.

A series of photos of the transition from rails to road carried out by the CDR in 1960. The scene is the Lifford Bridge. **Top left:** A goods train leaves Strabane round the curve for Lifford in the 1950s. **Middle left:** The same scene after the track was lifted and the trackbed paved. **Top right:** Walking along the overgrown track by Lifford Bridge. **Middle Right:** The same scene after the track removal. **Bottom:** One of the buses hired from CIE operating the replacement Strabane to Letterkenny bus service on the bridge. All photos from CDRRL archives.

VII

The Omnibuses

1960-71

The County Donegal's first foray into the operation of road buses in 1930, ended somewhat unhappily three years later as all four of the second-hand Reo buses it had purchased from the Great Northern Railway of Ireland had been reduced to scrap condition by the rudimentary state of the county's roads. With typical ingenuity, CDR Manager Henry Forbes had the two vehicles in the best condition converted into railcars! Fitted with 36hp Ford engines and numbered into the railcar series as nos. 9 and 10 this conversion gave the buses a new of lease of life. No.9 remained in service for a further 16 years although no.10 was destroyed in an accidental fire in 1939.

With almost total reliance on railcars for passenger duties after World War Two, the CDR did not turn its attention to road bus operations again until 1959 when it became clear that the rail services would have to be withdrawn. Beginning on the morning of January 1st, 1960, all CDR passenger services were handled by six P class Leyland buses which were hired from Córas Iompair Éireann.

These vehicles operated to the former rail timetable and followed the routes of the rail services. These

Above: A real railbus! Hired P-class Leyland P174 at Lifford Station platform undergoing the customs inspection while forming the 2.15pm Strabane to Letterkenny service. Photo from the Sam Carse collection - courtesy David Carse.

services were initially based at Strabane and served Stranorlar-Ballybofey, Donegal Town and Killybegs, while another route served Letterkenny. Ballyshannon lost its CDR link with Donegal Town at this stage as CIE buses ran between these two towns.

The P class Leylands had been in service with CIE for a number of years and proved reliable and popular with the crews. The six 39-seaters were adequate during the winter months but by June 1960 an extra four P class buses were hired to cope with the summer traffic. In an effort to retain its railway identity the company had the buses painted in their familiar red and cream livery and the CDR crest was displayed on the body sides. For a short time in 1960 buses leaving Strabane, in Co. Tyrone, entered Co. Donegal by crossing the River Foyle by the former railway bridge and ran along the trackbed as far as Lifford Station due to weight restrictions on the existing road bridge.

The P class had been introduced by CIE in 1949-59 and gave good service. Indeed, some were still in use as tow trucks in Dublin in 1991! The Donegal roads took their toll and in April and May 1965, the CDR bought six Leyland Tiger Cubs from the East Midland Road Car Co in Britain. These 44 seaters were completely mechanically overhauled at Stranorlar and the bodywork was refurbished by O'Doherty, coachbuilders of Strabane, who had previously contracted with the CDR to build railcar bodies.

The Tiger Cubs were never graced with fleet numbers and were identified by their British registration numbers which they retained throughout their service lives. These were: ORR321, ORR322, ORR331, ORR332, ORR333 and ORR 339.

Although the increase in seating capacity was of some help, extra vehicles continued to be hired for the summer seasons. By now CIE had introduced the E class, their version of the Leyland Leopard and, in December 1965, the first of these entered CDR service. It is worth noting that at this time CIE had forsaken its familiar green bus livery and the 'Flying Snail' emblem and adopted the red and cream colour scheme quite similar to the CDR colours.

It has been said that Stranorlar staff covered the new CIE emblem on some hired buses with the CDR crest and inevitably CIE were not very impressed. It is interesting to note that the last E class was withdrawn from CIE services around the early 1990s. Two of the E Class buses which operated on the CDR routes are now preserved. No E140 is at the Cavan & Leitrim Railway at Dromod, and E152 is housed in working order in Dublin. The latter did travel to Donegal Town for the CDRRL Open Day in 2003, when it ferried passengers from Donegal Town to take the preserved train at Fintown.

While passenger numbers dropped with the closure of the rail links between Strabane and Derry in 1965, there was obviously some long distance business to be gained as, in 1967, an express bus service between Killybegs and Belfast was inaugurated operated jointly with Ulsterbus. At first only one run in each direction was scheduled, with the Ulsterbus leaving Belfast at 8.30am and, after changing to a CDR vehicle at Strabane, passengers arrived at Killybegs at 1.30pm. The return service left Killybegs at 3pm and took almost five hours to reach Belfast.

After just one successful summer season the "Belfast Express'" frequency was increased to two trips each way with morning and afternoon departures from both Belfast and Killybegs. While Belfast is still a major point of entry for tourists and returning emigrants, on the Belfast and Larne boats and via Aldergrove and City airports, sadly there is no direct service on this route today.

The CDR's only other long distance run, also in conjunction with Ulsterbus, was the Letterkenny to Aldergrove (Belfast airport) Express but when this service was introduced in 1971 the CDR's days as an independent entity were numbered. ORR332, the last surviving Tiger Cub and the last bus owned by the CDR was pensioned off in December 1970, retiring to the seaside at Bundoran to spend its last days as a holiday home in company with ORR339.

By June 1971 the E class reigned supreme and signs of a CIE takeover were very much in evidence and when, on the 12th July, the CDR was officially absorbed into the national transport company little surprise was felt in the county.

The County Donegal Railway was one of the last railway companies in the British Isles to operate an independent road service. The honour of being the very last falls to the rival – the Londonderry and Lough Swilly Railway – which, affectionately known as "The Swilly", continued to operate services out of Derry along its old railway routes to Carndonagh, Letterkenny, Burtonport and many places in between right up to April 19th 2014, when another chapter of Irish transport heritage sadly closed.

Top: CDR motorman Mickey Lafferty, who transferred from railcars to the buses at the closure of the railway in 1959, stands proudly beside his Tiger Cub outside the Donegal Town goods shed in July 67.
Middle: Letterkenny Station platform and canopy in use as a bus wash area for ORR 331 in July 1966.
Bottom: The Killybegs-Belfast 'express' loads at Donegal Town in July 1970, driven by former railcar motorman, the late Collins Lafferty. Photos by Hugh Dougherty.

VIII

Road Freight Operations

Three years after the CDR's limited entry into road bus operations, four secondhand road lorries were acquired and goods transport began with distribution from the main railway stations. Profits from the road freight were first seen in 1936 and by the following year no less than 19 lorries were running, though 15 of these were obtained secondhand.

At first services were operated on an "as required' basis but in 1939 regular routes and schedules were introduced. Nine lorries were employed on seven routes. These were: 1. Stranorlar and West, 2. Castlefin, Raphoe, Convoy and Stranorlar local collections, 3. Lifford and Strabane cross-border shuttle, 4. Letterkenny Town and district, 6. Glenties, Ardara, Dungloe and Killybegs, and 7. Donegal County Council work.

During the 'Emergency' (as the Second World War was known in Ireland) difficulties were experienced in keeping a fleet on the road. Petrol was rationed and spares were scarce and, by 1943, the Joint Committee had reduced their fleet to eight vehicles.

Ground limestone, foodstuffs, agricultural requisites and County Council roadworks kept these lorries busy during the day and many saw evening service delivering turf as domestic fuel, coal, was in short supply.

Above: A line-up of CDR road haulage vehicles at Stranorlar, including a 1959 Leyland Hippo and 1951 Austin. Photo by the late Seamus Clerkin.

A number of secondhand trucks were acquired in 1944 and two buses bought from the Bogagh Bus Co, were converted to lorries by the ever helpful GNR(I) works at Dundalk. The end of the war brought improvements in the local economy and for the first time in 12 years new vehicles were purchased. In 1947 regular rail services on the Glenties branch ceased and road vehicles were substituted on the Glenties – Stranorlar route. Livestock began to play an important part in freight earnings about this time and sheep from the fairs at Brockagh and other villages were conveyed to Derry for shipment to Scotland.

The Donegal County Council roadwork kept a good portion of the fleet busy and by 1950 three agricultural tractors were also engaged in this work. At this time also, 1,900 tonnes of wheat were diverted by road from Strabane via St Johnstone providing an unexpected busy period for the fleet.

Although the CDR had introduced diesel railcars in 1933 there were no diesel lorries on the CDR books until 1954. The reason for the delay in introducing the more economical diesels was that it was felt that petrol-engined lorries had a higher top speed and this was important on the fish traffic run from Killybegs to the Dublin market.

The fish often left Killybegs quite late at night and, in order to reach Dublin by 6am, two drivers were assigned to each lorry, one driving while the other rested. The first fish on the market attracted the highest prices and the CDR drivers considered it a matter of pride to do well for the fishermen.

Two Leyland Comet diesel lorries were obtained in 1954 and these seemed to have paved the way for further diesels as four Bedford 7-ton tipping trucks soon followed and these were all powered by Perkins P6 diesel engines. The 7-tonners were too heavy for the prevailing road conditions and were replaced after only two years by 5 ton Bedford tipper trucks.

In 1955 the first articulated tractor unit was introduced. This Bedford Scammel diesel (fleet no.67) was used on the Derry-Letterkenny petrol tankers at first but, by the following year, a similar contract between Derry and Killybegs had been won and two more tractor units were purchased. The three units were also employed on the haulage of 2,000 tons of cast iron water pipes from Derry to all parts of the CDR area and the Joint Committee won approval to use one-man operated 40-foot trailers before CIE (the national carrier) received similar authorisation.

In 1956 a Ford Thames two ton box van was brought into service on the Lifford and Letterkenny mail run replacing one railcar working and, by the time of the withdrawal of the rail services in 1959, a large number of Ford Thames trader box vans were in use and the mail services were switched from rail to road without interruption.

From the late 1950s vehicles of larger tonnage were acquired in preparation for the road-only freight service and Leyland Super Comets, Leyland Hippos and AEC matadors came into use. The late Sam Carse has recorded the 1964 lorry receipts which give an indication of the type of traffic carried in the years after the withdrawal of rail services; ground limestone - £16,000, fish - £9,313, petrol and oil - £10,356, livestock - £433, and coal traffic - £288.

The CDR lorries remained a familiar sight on Donegal roads until CIE absorbed the company in 1971 and several of the vehicles were taken into the CIE fleet and carried both their new CIE and old CDR numbers.

Top: Obviously new to the fleet, a sparkling Leyland Super Comet ZP6080 takes a load of empty fish boxes to Stranorlar in May 1959. **Middle:** Two CDR tractor units in action at the Diamond, Donegal Town. The oversized loads appear to be bound for the fish meal plant at Killybegs, though the date is not known. The leading tractor carries Northern Ireland registration and the Bedford Tractor, behind, was new in 1955. **Bottom:** A selection of CDR lorries at Stranorlar in the 1960s. All three photos by the late Seamus Clerkin.

Upper: Bedford Scammell tractor No 6 at Letterkenny. This unit was bought with the Derry to Letterkenny petrol traffic in mnd although it did haul flat trailers at times. Photo from the Sam Carse collection - courtesy David Carse. **Lower:** Bedford 7-ton tipping lorry no 70. A number of these were bought by the CDR in 1955 but were found to be unsuitable for the Donegal roads and some were replaced by 1957. Photo from the CDRRL archives.

Above: Derelict road and rail vehicles including Coach No 29 at Stranorlar, 1957. Photo by N C Simmons, Photos From The Fifties..

Left: Railcars 16 (left) and 12 (cab only visible) at Donegal Town after tracklifting, around September 1960. It is likely that the passenger trailer attached to Railcar 16 is that of No 15 which has now been restored at Donegal Town station in 2013. In the picture are, l to r, Anthony Timoney (CDR driver), Hugh (The Dodger) O'Donnell (mail van driver), and Jimmy Grant (dec) who was a CDR clerk. Photo by the late Gerry McAuley.

Below: Having served its time on the tracklifting project in 1960, Railcar 12 is moved away to future security through Donegal Town by road, using a CDR lorry of course. Photo from CDRRL archives.

Above: Fitter McGilloway services the fuel metering pumps of the power bogie of Railcar No 12 at Stranorlar Depot in 1954. Photo by the late Seamus Clerkin. **Below:** The CDRJC's clerical staff at Stranorlar in the 1950s. Front row, left to right - Bernard McGinty, chief clerk (deceased); Kathleen Meenhan/McGinty, clerk; John McCusker, clerk; Raymond Curran; Peg Dunion/O'Flaherty, clerk; Ross Parks, clerical officer, (deceased); Back row, left to right - John P Maher, clerical officer (deceased), R P Dunion, clerical officer (deceased); Gerard McDermot, clerical officer. Photo by J Quinn, Ballybofey

Top: A Class 5A loco undergoing minor repairs on shed at Stranorlar in 1957. Photo by N C Simmons, from Photos From The Fifties.. **Above:** The new fish pier at Killybegs as rebuilt in 1952 complete with a line of CDR rails which are still in situ in the 21st century, over 50 years after the railway closed. Photo by the late J C Gillham.

Above: Donegal Town with Class 5 loco *Meenglas* about to attach three further coaches - 17, 56 & 47 from left to right - to the very last Ancient Order of Hibernians special from Strabane to Killybegs, Saturday 15th August 1959. Photo by John Langford.

IX

Climb Aboard!

Let us take a trip now on the County Donegal Railway. It's late spring in 1952 and of course we are in possession of a pass that will take us over all parts of the system.

We start our tour of the CDR as many tourists did at the southernmost terminus; Ballyshannon. The station here is not far from the town's largest church and is about one mile and across the River Erne from the GNR(I)'s station on the Bundoran branch.

Climbing aboard, our journey on Railcar No 18 takes us past the halt and pier at Creevy, over undulating countryside and, as the sea sparkles off to our left, we approach Rossnowlagh. This is a seaside resort, having no village as such but a large hotel (still open in 2015), a long sandy beach and some caravan parks. To the CDR, Rossnowlagh is a major destination for the 12th of July Orange Order specials.

Continuing northwards we go then towards Ballintra, at one time the staff interchange on the branch. A staff interchange on a single-line railway like the CDR is usually at a station and consists of a short section of double track allowing trains from the opposite directions to pass. The 'staff' is a special stick which the engine driver must receive from the signalman indicating that there is no other train on the single-line track ahead and that he may proceed to the next passing point.

The goods store at Ballintra was knocked down in 1949 and now little activity greets our passing.

Turning inland the tracks take us to Laghy station just outside the village of the same name and, again, all is quiet, so we continue towards Donegal town, the tracks winding to follow the edges of the low hills.

We travel first along embankments then through a deep cutting until we pass the Hospital Halt just outside Donegal itself. There was a fatal accident here in August 1949 when a steam locomotive on a goods train from Ballyshannon collided with a railcar – an instance when the security of the 'staff' section system failed to prevent disaster.

Travelling under the adjacent road bridge, which carries the main Donegal to Ballybofey road, we next cross over the River Eske and our branch line joins the main Stranorlar line as we run in to Donegal station.

Here we leave the railcar and, checking the timetable, we find that we have forty minutes to wait before catching the 9.10am to Killybegs. Almost immediately after our arrival in Railcar No 18, another railcar towing a trailer pulls out from the other platform en route to Stabane and we go up on to the iron open-trellis footbridge for a better view of the departure.

To our right a class 5 steam engine is busily involved in some early morning shunting near the goods shed and, after watching for a while, we go to the Easons newsstand on the platform to buy a morning paper from Maggie Walsh. Adjoining the station building is the stationmaster's house with its three gables, the last one of which was added in 1924.

At 9.10am exactly we board our railcar for Killybegs. This time we are to travel in Railcar No 20, the most modern vehicle on the "Donegal' and we find it comfortable though the faint odour of diesel fuel is not exactly welcomed and we are thankful that we ate breakfast in Ballyshannon! The starter signal moves downwards to the 'Off' position, our railcar leaves the platform and we pass over the level crossing and soon enter a cutting as we head towards Killymard Halt.

Beyond Killymard the diesel engine labours as we charge the one and a half mile long Glen Bank, which plunged under the high bridge carrying the old main road before coming to a stop at Mountcharles, having covered the four miles from Donegal in 15 minutes. The crane at Mountcharles can lift up to five tons and is the sole reminder of the once important traffic in local stone from this station.

After our railcar restarts we pass through mainly agricultural land and wave at a few workers in their fields. Occasional glimpses of Donegal bay and the Sligo mountains beyond are caught before we pass Doorin Road Halt and then cross the River Eany by a metal bridge just before entering Inver Station.

Water is taken here to top up a leaky radiator and we chat for a moment to the station master until the railcar is ready and again moves on through the countryside, crossing the road at Cannons and then Battles Cross until the sea comes into view again and a tiny harbour of Inver Port. Here we catch a glimpse of our friends, the McHugh brothers, preparing for the day's lobster fishing.

The sea stays with us most of the way to Dunkineely Station and, after a short stop here, we begin the hard curving climb up to Bruckless. From here on until we are in sight of Killybegs the track winds through differing terrains – farmland and bog – and the beech trees at the lineside often restrict our view.

At last we run into Killybegs with the waters of the harbour, one of the safest natural harbours on Ireland's western seaboard, lapping against the embankment to our left.

Killybegs station itself is unlike the cottage-style buildings at Mountcharles, Inver and Dunkineely, but it bears a striking resemblance to that of Donegal town though it possesses only two gables and has an overall roof covering most of the passenger platform – a blessing in winter months. We have quite some time to spend here before our return train so we walk along a siding running down to the pier where coal dust lies in evidence to a recent visit by a collier. Wagons can be moved onto the pier for loading from the ships though one fears that a loco might prove too heavy for the hardwood piles. The track still exists on the pier in 2015 though all other trace of the railway has gone. We take refreshment at the Bayview Hotel and, suitably fortified, we return to the station to catch the 12.55pm back to Donegal.

Back at Donegal again at 2.10pm we have three minutes to change platforms and board our train to Stranorlar. This time we will be carried in Railcar No 10, which was built in 1932 for the Clogher Valley Railway, and we rattle our way out of the station, past the turnout of the Ballyshannon branch, through the trees towards Clar.

Passing under the road at Clar Bridge we climb and twist along before crossing the road again, this time by a level crossing to reach Lough Eske station and post office. At one time this was as close to Donegal Town as the railway could get and the station was then known as Druminnin. Lough Eske itself lies to the north – a vast expanse of tree-lined water famed for its salmon and dotted with tiny islands.

Donegal Town Station on 15th August 1959. Class 5 loco *Meenglas* prepares to leave from the island platform on the right with the return AOH Special - the very last one - from Killybegs to Strabane at about 8.25pm while Railcar No 18 waits at the main platform. CDRJC General Manager Bernard Curran strides towards the photographer. Photo by John Langford.

Lough Eske Station on a Friday evening in August 1959. The 8.4pm goods from Donegal To Stranorlar headed by *Meenglas* has paused for the crew to take tea. The train consists of 5-compartment coach no 12, grey goods van no 7, and 3rd-brake-3rd coach no 28, which will later survive the railway's closure and be restored at Donegal Town. Photo by John Langford.

On leaving the station we meet a long passing loop and, just for a moment, there is the illusion of a double track railway before the single line again stretches ahead pointing towards the magnificent Blue Stack Mountains. This imposing façade is split by a deep valley and it is towards this that No 10 takes us, climbing laboriously all the while.

The valley between the peaks of Croaghconnellagh and Croonagh is the Barnesmore Gap, a much favoured haunt in former times of the highwaymen and brigands. Passing Barnesmore Halt the gradient becomes severe and to the left we see the famous Biddy O'Barnes public house before we enter the Gap itself on a rock-cut ledge high above the road. In the early days of the railway the winds in the Gap actually brought steam trains to a standstill on some occasions but our journey is accompanied by brilliant sunshine and the occasional startled screech of a peregrine.

Once out of Barnesmore Gap we pause for a moment at Derg Bridge Halt in open moorland then we run alongside Lough Mourne and plunge through the cutting towards the halt at Meenglass, which was built for the convenience of Lord Lifford who lived in nearby Meenglass Castle. Beyond the halt we cross a bridge over the road at Seissiaghoneill and then over the River Finn on a magnificent viaduct before curving into Stranorlar Station at ten past three.

Stranorlar is the main station on the CDR's system and houses the maintenance and management facilities. Several carriages dating from 1901 and 1907 lie around awaiting scrapping and, in contrast, three gleaming coaches – just bought second-hand from the Northern Counties Committee's Ballycastle line – sit outside the carriage shed for their next turn of duty on the Sunday excursion trains.

Our imaginary pass allows us to visit the engine sheds and workshops before a few words with Mr Curran, the railway's manager, confirm that we are to be allowed a special privilege and can ride in the brake van on one of the last goods specials to traverse the Glenties line.

The line to Glenties was closed to passengers in 1947 though the occasional freight train is run if required and, shortly after crossing the River Finn on an impressive girder bridge with the track running beside the river we become aware of lush grass growing between the rails. Nature is reclaiming its rights along the way and, as we pass through Glenmore and Cloghan the driver must constantly resort to the sanders to keep a firm grip on the grassy rail. The sanders consist of a reservoir of dry sand on the front of the locomotive together with a series of pipes leading to a point just in front of the driving wheels. The driver just has to pull a small lever to release a steady flow of sand onto the rails to help the wheels grip.

Our train consists mainly of empty cattle wagons and is hauled by class 4 steam locomotive no.11 *Erne*. We are travelling in the brake van which is brake no. 23 built in 1893 and Willy the guard is regaling us with many stories of the line and its people. We scarcely notice the view until we are on the shores of beautiful Lough Finn, a long narrow lake at the foot of Aghla mountain.

Stopping for a while at Fintown station we are again amazed at how fast the signs of railway activity are disappearing into the undergrowth. After taking a breather for a while Erne makes a slippery start from Fintown and we head through the bogs to a halt at Shallogans where we begin to climb again and cross the Owenea River twice in rapid succession on stone-built viaducts, still in good condiiton in 2015, at a place known as the Banna Bui and we finally come into the station of Glenties.

CDR lorries and a GNR bus parked at the station remind us that the train is an invader here nowadays and as we chat with Danny Boyle who lived in the station house we wonder just how long the remains of the railway will last because even these rare goods workings are due to stop soon. An overnight stay in Glenties – at the Highlands Hotel perhaps – is recommended as the sun is getting low, the turf rises into the still air and the evening's entertainment is beginning in the village pubs.

On the second day of our tour we take the GNR bus from Glenties to Stranorlar and arrive there just in time to board the 9.31am for Strabane. In contrast to the overgrown Glenties branch the ballast on this route is very clean and hardly a blade of grass is seen between the rails as the track follows a gentle slope towards Castlefin. At Liscooly we encounter the only level crossing on this line and, twenty minutes after leaving Stranorlar, Castlefin is reached. At the far platform the CDR's unique diesel shunter,

Phœnix, stands with five grey vans – probably awaiting customs examination – and we take a quick look at the train during our five-minute stopover.

A mile and a half further on we pass Clady station and then cross the River Finn at Urney bridge. Another river crossing is made just before we pull into Strabane Station.

We are now in Northern Ireland. Customs examination takes only a few minutes and we are then free to take a look around. Most of the buildings here are yellow brick and the main platforms are linked by a footbridge. This station is used by both the five foot three inch gauge Great Northern Railway (Ireland) and the three foot gauge CDR and, after the only two days on the narrow gauge, the sight of one of the GNR 4-4-0 locos is strange and the engine seems unusually large.

We wander down to take a brief look at the dual gauge turntable and then sip a welcome cup of tea before taking the railcar to Letterkenny at ten past eleven. Not far out from Strabane our railcar stops at Lifford where there is some delay as post office and railway staff, to the accompaniment of shouts of 'Killybegs 2', 'Donegal 4', and so on, remove many bags of mail from the small red wagon we have in tow. Lifford has the post office sorting depot and the mail from all stations on the line is brought here.

Taking aboard only two bags of mail for Letterkenny we set off again and pass Ballindrait and Coolaghy before calling at Raphoe. This is a pretty town and a few passengers alight here to visit the cathedral.

After Raphoe, Convoy is reached – a small town with a large mill providing plenty of goods traffic for which an extra large (surviving) goods shed was built. There then follows a stiff climb at 1 in 50 before our railcar coasts the remaining eight miles into Letterkenny. Here we leave the CDR station and visit the Londonderry and Lough Swilly Railway's yard. Swilly road buses and trucks are much in evidence and it is rumoured that rail services on the Swilly lines will be withdrawn next year and the buses and lorries will then carry all the traffic.

At 2.45pm we take our train back to Strabane to catch a connection to Derry over the last stretch of CDR track in our tour. This section lies entirely within Northern Ireland and railcars do not venture onto this part of the line. Our short train behind class 5 locomotive no.6 Columbkille takes us through fertile countryside, very different from that encountered on the Stranorlar to Donegal and Glenties lines and the occasional glimpse of a red pillar box or telephone kiosk reinforces the knowledge that we have crossed an international border.

We are nearing Donemana. It was here in 1913 that a Sunday train returning from Derry to Strabane entered the passing loop at 40mph, despite a 6mph speed restriction, and left the rails. One person was killed in this accident and intoxication of the loco crew was thought to be to blame.

From Donemana we climb towards Desertone and swing towards the banks of the River Foyle. The gradient falls until we reach the river and follow its course into Derry. Across the river, the GNR line to Strabane duplicates our route and we pull into the red brick Victoria Road station. In Derry we leave the County Donegal Railway and as there are rail termini in this city belonging to the Great Northern Railway, the LMS (Northern Counties Commission) and the Londonderry and Lough Swilly Railway, we can take our time and explore more of Ireland's rich railway scenery.

Left: Donemana looking north in December 1955, after the track had been lifted. **Right.** Desertone looking north in May 1955 before the last train had passed, a school special to Derry in June 1955. Both photos by Michael Bunch.

Upper: Letterkenny in the 1930s. **Middle:** Killybegs in the early years of the 20th Century. The rails curve off the wooden planked fish pier in a sharp rightward turn to join the lines to the oil depot and then on to the station beyond the right-hand edge of the photo. The rails are still in situ in 2015 in the more modern fish pier and are therefore the last remnant of the CDRJC's "route" that remains in place. **Lower:** Raphoe, on 17th Sept 1957. The unidentified engine of the 8.10am Strabane to Letterkenny goods is attaching a van to the rear of the 8.45am Letterkenny to Strabane railcar which is already hauling a coach. Note the 3rd-brake-3rd coach to the left of the loco and that the far signal is "off". All the above from the John Langford collection.

X

The Survivors

When the County Donegal Railways Joint Committee finally withdrew all rail services on December 31st 1959 railway preservation was unknown in Ireland. In Wales, the narrow-gauge Talyllyn Railway had been operated by enthusiasts for almost a decade, and in Sussex in the south of England the standard gauge Bluebell Railway was also growing at the hands of volunteers.

There was little interest in such pursuits however in the west of Ireland and one would have expected that the CDR locomotives and rolling stock would face the scrap man's hammer – a fate which had accounted for every Swilly, Clogher Valley and LMS (NCC) narrow gauge locomotive. Surprisingly, due to three separate and unusual purchasers at the disposal sales, a wealth of Donegal rail vehicles survive to be enjoyed today.

With the closure of the CDR there remained only one narrow gauge railway in Ireland: the 48-mile long West Clare Railway (WCR) operated by CIE. Modernisation in 1952 had left the WCR equipped with Walker railcars identical to the CDR nos. 19 and 20 and it would have made sense if they had been bought by the WCR to augment their fleet. However, it was clear by this time that the West Clare would not last long and no formal offer was made.

The Isle of Man Railway

Interest in the CDR's most modern railcars came across the Irish Sea, from the Isle of Man Railway Company, who operated the only remaining operational three-foot gauge railway in the British isles, now still run as a nationalised industry by the Isle of Man government. The company's interest in the railcars was for exactly the same reason that Henry Forbes had introduced them to the County Donegal many years before - to provide a fast, comfortable passenger service at less than the cost of steam operations.

On the Isle of Man the peak time for rail operations was and is during the holiday season of July and August, though a healthy domestic traffic was evident all year round on certain routes in the early years.

Railcars 19 and 20 were bought at the public auction in Stranorlar on March 1st, 1961 at a cost of £160 each and were subsequently dismantled and moved to Derry for a further charge of £165. Shipment from Derry to the Isle of Man cost an extra £250 and they were placed aboard the coaster MV Antrim Coast on May 6th in the charge of Burns Laird Shipping and were unloaded at Douglas IoM the following day.

Overhauls and modifications were carried out at Douglas and trials were carried out on the Peel line, and between Douglas and Port Erin (this latter being the only section of track on the Isle of Man Railway still open today).

The railcars entered traffic in 1962 and were used on both summer tourist traffic and the winter domestic services. On the Isle of Man 19 and 20 operated 'back to back', thereby reducing the need for turntables and, by the late '60s, some workings on permanent way maintenance trains were added to their schedule.

The railcars do not appear to have been marshalled into steam-hauled trains very often as the couplings on the power bogies were not made compatible with other Isle of Man stock until 1984. The rear couplings remain at Donegal height. The original CDR numbers are retained though their passenger workings were reduced until 1989. From September of that year, nos. 19 and 20 were restricted to shunting duties with the occasional permanent way or maintenance train and rare enthusiasts' special workings. These two cars are currently partially restored awaiting further funds, and stored inside at Douglas Station.

The Ulster Folk & Transport Museum, Cultra

In 1960 the original Belfast Transport Museum moved from its old quarters at the old motor sheds of the Belfast and County Down Railway to new premises at Witham Street, Belfast, and began to expand its collection. The collection is now housed in the splendid museum at Cultra, east of Belfast.

The narrow gauge exhibits include a number of CDR vehicles: Class 5A locomotive No 2 *Blanche*, the unique diesel tractor *Phœnix*, Railcar No 1, the ex-Dublin & Blessington Tramway Railcar Trailer No 3. and the ex-Clogher Valley Railway Railcar No 10. Cultra also has the directors' saloon Coach No 1, and open wagon No 136.

A Visit From The Dentist

The majority of the rest of the surviving CDR stock was saved from immediate extinction by the intervention from a most unexpected source. During World War Two an American dentist, Dr Ralph Cox, entered the US Air Force and became a pilot. When hostilities ceased Dr Cox is reported to have bought several surplus aeroplanes and set up an airline. In the air travel boom years of the 1950s there were fortunes to be made and the ex-dentist became a wealthy man. Another of the good dentist's interests was steam railways and he dreamed of opening one of these in Wildwood, New Jersey, USA.

At two sales of surplus County Donegal Railway stock the American purchased 100 tons of rails, 10 tons of points (switches in US railway parlance) and signal rodding, two turntables, a signal cabin, and the Stranorlar platform canopy. In addition, four steam locomotives: *Meenglas*, *Drumboe*, *Columbkille* and *Erne*, three railcars: nos. 12, 16 and 18, ten passenger coaches and a total of 54 goods vehicles, were acquired.

Much of the rolling stock was repainted and, to some degree, refurbished after the purchase and lay at Stranorlar (*Columbkille* and the railcars),

Letterkenny (*Erne*) and Strabane (*Meenglas*, *Drumboe* and the coaches) awaiting transport to the USA. It appears that Dr Cox's airline went into liquidation about this time and he had to abandon his plans to build his railway.

At Stranorlar most items were stored in the old railway sheds, but at Strabane and Letterkenny stock lay out in the open. At Strabane the two locos and rolling stock were effectively guarded by the GNR operation which was still running in the early 1960s. Photos confirm that the stock even received a coat of paint at that time. However, after closure of the GNR line through Strabane in February 1965, vandals and the Irish weather began to take their toll on the coaches and locos. At Strabane Drumboe and *Meenglas* lost any part that could be removed and the coaches had all their windows smashed. Columbkille and Railcar no.12 were stored indoors undamaged at Stranorlar though by 1972 CIE were anxious that they should be removed.

In Derry a group of enthusiasts formed the North-West of Ireland Railway Society (NWIRS) in an effort to preserve the remaining CDR vehicles and, in the early '70s, took possession of Columbkille and railcars nos. 12 and 18 and moved them to the old CDR station at Victoria Road.

This location was intended to be the starting point for a short length of track to Prehen and a museum was set up. As late as 1977 quotations were being received for the shipping of Dr Cox's stock to New York but a price of £31,000 may well have persuaded him to leave his purchases in Ireland.

The future was not totally bright for the NWIRS however, because in 1978 the Victoria Road terminal was sold and a new home had to be found. The CDR stock was moved to Shanes Castle Railway, a small 1.5 mile-long tourist railway in the estate of Lord O'Neill in Co. Antrim, and remained there for some years, thanks to the generous support of Lord O'Neill himself.

Derry City Council was also interested in railway preservation and, in May 1989, a magnificent new building, the Foyle Valley Railway Centre, was opened on the site of the old GNR(I) terminus in Foyle Road. The stock was returned from Shanes Castle and Meenglas and *Drumboe* were also rescued from Strabane where they had fallen into a terrible state of repair.

Locomotive *Columbkille*, Coach 14, Red Van 19, and Railcar 12 were all stored in the new building where they remain to this day. *Meenglas* was stored outside and also remains in place, and for most of the time has appeared weathered and uncared for, although it does receive the occasional coat of paint.

For a period in the 1990s Railcar 18 was also stored at the Foyle Valley Railway Centre, and trips were run for tourists and visitors using Railcars 12 and 18 running back-to-back on three foot gauge track laid for some two miles towards Carrigans in a co-operative effort by Derry City Council and NWIRS. During this time, Coach 30 was also restored, though not quite to its original appearance.

Arguments arose about the actual ownership of some of the surviving items and the means of managing the Centre and the train rides. Unfortunately this led to the closure of the Centre shortly after the Millenium. Today the Foyle Valley Railway Centre line along the old GNR(I) line beside the river has been out of use for a decade and will need relaying if it is to be used for passenger trips again. However the museum has opened from time to time for visitors to see the exhibits. In March 2015 Derry City Council decided to close the Centre and seek new tenants or promoters, who hopefully will revive the operation.

Meanwhile it was established that NWIRS were owners of Railcar 18 and this was removed in running order to the Fintown Railway (see below) where it is still used in summer services and on special occasions.

South Donegal Railway Restoration Society

While enthusiasts across the border had been active, there was little to satisfy railway fans in Co. Donegal, the original home of the railway, until January 1991. Then, as a result of two well attended public meetings, the South Donegal Railway Restoration Society was formed. The original brief was to investigate if any sections of the former CDR's trackbed could be reopened for tourist use and to secure at least some original CDR rolling stock to work the line.

The choice was eventually narrowed down to two options: an eight mile stretch on the Glenties branch, between Glenties and Fintown, or 9.2 miles on the Donegal to Stranorlar route from Meenglas Halt to Barnesmore Halt, passing through the Barnesmore Gap. In July 1991 it was decided to pursue the restoration of the Barnesmore line as this appeared to offer greater commercial viability. Unfortunately the scheme was thwarted by a last minute announcement by the County Council to construct a bypass along part of the route east of Lough Mourne and geological problems at the foot of the Barnesmore Gap. So far, up to 2015, the bypass has never appeared.

Meanwhile, in April 1991, by arrangement with the NWIRS, locomotive *Drumboe* was loaned to the South Donegal Railway Restoration Society for restoration, and was brought back to the twin-towns of Ballybofey-Stranorlar on a low-loader. Local business provided sponsorship to cover transport costs and *Drumboe*, in very poor condition after over a quarter of a century in the open at Strabane, awaited repair work, which did not begin until Interreg grant aid allowed this in 2006.

The Society was able to occupy the old Station House in Donegal Town as its headquarters and to establish a railway heritage centre.

In May 1991, Society committee member Dave Bell discovered two CDR vehicles at a caravan park in Dunfanaghy, Co Donegal. These were a brake third, one of the 1893 batch from Oldbury's, and the passenger cabin of Railcar No 15 (originally thought to be 14). The former underwent a restoration programmein 1994/5 but the latter had to await a grant from Donegal Local Development Company in 2012 before its body was rebuilt, see page 4.

One other item collected by The Society was the body of railcar trailer 5, whose reincarnation is covered on page 61.

The Fintown Railway

After the bypass announcement seemed to put paid to the idea of returing the railway to Barnesmore Gap, a group of SDRRS members set up the Fintown railway to exercise the option between Fintown and Glenties. Due to the excellent condition of the trackbed (lttle short of amazing after 40 years of neglect) and the enthusiasm of the group leaders, especially Joseph Brennan, track was laid quickly for a short distance from Fintown and trains were run using a locotractor and ex-Belgian tramcars as passenger units.

Although the location has great beauty, its remoteness has an effect on the attraction of visitors. Nonetheless, the railway has already managed to survive for almost twenty years. The arrival of Railcar 18 was a boost and the track extends now for some three miles from Fintown towards Glenties. At the time of writing the railway opens in the summer months for rides in Railcar 18, and these are supplemented by services for Hallowe'en and Santa Specials. There is still the dream of eventually reaching Glenties.

County Donegal Railway Restoration Ltd

In 2002, the South Donegal Railway Restoration Society was wound up and a new company formed - County Donegal Railway Restoration Ltd (CDRRL) - in order to avail itself of job creation grants under the Government's Social Economy Scheme. This scheme assisted employment costs, thereby improving the sustainability of running the Donegal Railway Heritage Centre established in the old station in Donegal Town and supporting the pursuit of establishing a working railway. Unfortunately the last few years have seen a major reduction in tourists to the Donegal region which has reduced income significantly, but nevertheless the company has managed to break even but only through strenuous efforts by the management at the Centre.

Since 2005, the company has been particularly successful in securing grants to restore the bodies of Railcar Trailer 5, Railcar Passenger Trailer 15, and ex-NCC luxury coach 58. These have been completed and are now accessible by visitors to the Donegal Railway Heritage Centre..

An Interreg IIIA grant allowed substantial restoration of locomotive *Drumboe* (see front cover) while a heritage grant allowed the collection and stabilisation of surviving wagons and stock. The company has also produced archive films on DVD as well as running a successful mail order business in books and related material. This book is itself part of a programme of several books with new material to be produced on the railways of County Donegal, and it is also hoped to produce further DVDs.

During 2009, as part of the preparation to commemorate the 50th anniversary of closure, CDRRL obtained permission to lay some 100 metres of 3-foot gauge track on the orignal trackbed beside local member Mervyn Johnson's restored crossing cottage at Mullanboys, near Inver. CDRRL's 4-seater motorised Wickham trolley, restored under the Interreg IIIA grant, was used for motive power, see below. Many visitors came including the Mayor of Donegal Town, even in the snowy weather (below), to sample this piece of the original line and it was hoped the resulting Press coverage would assist future Barnesmore Gap deliberations.

Provision of public access to the restored rolling stock at Donegal Town Station has considerably increased the size of the museum and consequently full size coach parties and groups can be handled. This includes facilities for special needs groups, and all displays can be reached by wheelchair.

The company has not forgotten the Barnesmore Gap scheme, and still hopes that there will be ways in the future of addressing the problems which befell the original scheme.

Although the museum itself is much expanded, the last few years have seen teams from the company travelling to other venues to run model railway shows, normally including a substantial proportion of layouts with scale County Donegal and Swilly models. This has brought valuable income to the Centre during times when visitor numbers to Donegal Town itself have been disappointingly low. This activity has also spread the reputation of the Centre and introduced the County Donegal Railway to many more people, whose younger generations never knew the railway itself.

The remaining County Donegal Railway stock and where to see it

Foyle Valley Railway Centre, Foyle Road, Derry, Northern Ireland

Outside:
Class 5 loco *Meenglas*

Inside:
Class 5 loco *Columbkille*
Railcar No 12 (operational)
Coaches No 14 and No 30
Red Wagon No 19
Swilly Coach Body
Swilly crane

**Donegal Railway Heritage Centre
The Old Station House
Tyrconnell St
Donegal Town, Co Donegal**
Tel 00 353 (0)74 9722655 - See more at
www.donegalrailway.com

Outside:
Coach 28
Railcar Trailer 5
Grey Van 84
Red Van Body 12
Newtowncunningham Signal Box
Railcar Passenger Unit No 15 (body only)
Coach 58 (body only)

Fintown Railway, Fintown, Co Donegal
Railcar No 18 (operational)

**Ulster Folk & Transport Museum, Cultra
Holywood, Co Down, BT18 0EU**
Tel: +44 (0) 28 9042 8428 - See more at:
http://www.nmni.com
Class 5A loco *Blanche*
Railcars Nos 1 & 10
Railcar Trailer 3
Phœnix No 11
Director's Saloon Coach No 1
Open Wagon No 136

**Railway Preservation Society of Ireland
Whitehead Excursion Station, Castleview Rd
Whitehead, Co Antrim BT38 9NA**

Outside:
Class 5 loco *Drumboe* (dismantled, partly restored)
Grey Van 30

**Isle of Man Railway
Douglas Station, Douglas, Isle of Man**

Inside:
Railcars 19 & 20, partly restored but not in use.

Bibliography

Bus Services of the County Donegal Railways, Hugh Dougherty, Transport Research Associates, Dublin 1972
The County Donegal Railways, Edward M Patterson, David & Charles, Newton Abbot, 1962, reprinted 1969,
    1982, revised with additional material by Joe Begley and Steve Flanders in 2014
The Lough Swilly Railway, Edward M Patterson, David & Charles, Newton Abbot, 1962, revised 1988
The Irish Narrow Gauge Railway, J D C A Prideaux, David & Charles, Newton Abbot, 1981
The County Donegal Railway, A Visitor's Guide, by Joe Begley, Dave Bell, Steve Flanders & Dave White, CDRRS
The Londonderry & Lough Swilly Railway, A Visitor's Guide, by Dave Bell & Steve Flanders. CDRRS
The Last Years of the Wee Donegal, Robert Robotham, Colourpoint, Newtownards, 1998
The Wee Donegal Revisited, Robert Robotham and Joe Curran, Colourpoint, Newtownards, 2002
The County Donegal Railways Companion, Roger Crombleholme, Midland, Hinckley, 2005
One Hundred and Fifty Years of Irish Railways, Fergus Mulligan, Appletree Press, Belfast, 1983, reprinted 1990
County Donegal Railway Wagons 1906 – 1959, S J Carse, Journal of the Irish Railway Record Society, 1976
CDRJC Coaching Stock, S J Carse, Journal of the Irish Railway Record Society, 1980
Motive Power on the CDR, Parts 1 and 2, S J Carse, Journal of the Irish Railway Record Society, 1987
Modelling the Irish Narrow Gauge, David Lloyd, Peco Publications, Seaton, 1989
The Starter, Journal of the NWIRS, Issues Nos 3 & 6 (1977/78) and Volume 2, Nos 1 & 2 (1991)
The Railway Magazine, March 1900, August 1912, May 1948, May 1950, February 1961 and March 1961
The Locomotive Magazine, 1902
Railway World magazine, December 1956
The Locomotive Encyclopædia, Robert Tufnell
The Phœnix, the magazine of County Donegal Railway Restoration Ltd, Issues 1-35
CDRJC Public Timetables, 1952 to 1959
CDRJC Special Instructions to Railcar Drivers, Henry Forbes, 1934
Official Railway Map of Ireland, The Railway Clearing House, London, 1927

Other Recommended Reading
Irish Steam, O S Nock, David & Charles, Newton Abbot, 1982
The Country Railway, David St John Thomas, David & Charles, Newton Abbot, 1976, reprinted 1983
Irish Railway Album, C P Boocock, Ian Allen Ltd, London, 1968

INDEX

ACKNOWLEDGEMENTS

Every effort was made to recontact photographers whose work was used in the first edition and any amendments they required to the captions for this edition duly made. Where no contact could be made, we have given credit and grateful acknowledgement as per the first edition. Thanks are also due to Mrs Ann Romain, wife of a previous CDRRL Chairman, who kindly typed into MS Word the original script using a copy of the First Edition, and to John Langford who proof-read the amended text and captions for this second edition.

The Life Story of Trailer 5

Originally supplied to the CDR in 1929 with a 28-seat body by O'Doherty's of Strabane with roof storage. This was later was removed and the running height raised to match other CDR vehicles. Trailer 5 lasted until the end of services, and was auctioned off in 1961 to become the changing room at Donegal Football Ground.

Top left & right: Trailer 5 in use on the railway before (left) and after roof rack removal and raising of the ride height. Photos by Michael Bunch.

Upper Left: By 1965, it was in use as a caravan at in Rossnowlagh. Photo by Des McGlynn.

Upper Right: After being moved from Rossnowlagh, Trailer 5 is seen derelict at Doochary after use as a holiday home. CDRRL archives.

Lower left & right: The RPSI restoration team at Whitehead has Trailer 5 ready to return to Donegal in May 2007. The interior shows the recuperated bus seating tried out but found to be too wide.

Bottom Left: The 4mm scale Donegal Town layout inside Trailer 5 at the August Bank Holiday show in 2013. Last three Photos by Neil Tee.

Left: The coach 58 skeleton after fitting of shaped hardwood uprights using an LMS template supplied by the RPSI.

Middle: After completion of the interior in May 2013, here is a full house watching the play "On The Camel's Hump". The doorway at rear is the "corridor" connection through to the passenger section of Railcar 15.

Lower: A view along the side of Coach 58 as completed - a far cry from the two derelict halves of the original that presented themselves to the restoration team only a year before. All three photos by Neil Tee.